The Development of Equity Capital Markets in Transition Economies

Contributions to Economics

Christoph M. Schneider
Research and Development Management: From the Soviet Union to Russia
1994. ISBN 3-7908-0757-5

Bernhard Böhm/Lionello F. Punzo (Eds.)
Economic Performance
1994. ISBN 3-7908-0811-3

Lars Olof Persson/Ulf Wiberg
Microregional Fragmentation
1995. ISBN 3-7908-0855-5

Ernesto Felli/Furio C. Rosati/ Giovanni Tria (Eds.)
The Service Sector: Productivity and Growth
1995. ISBN 3-7908-0875-X

Giuseppe Munda
Multicriteria Evaluation in Fuzzy Environment
1995. ISBN 3-7908-0892-X

Giovanni Galizzi/ Luciano Venturini (Eds.)
Economics of Innovation: The Case of Food Industry
1996. ISBN 3-7908-0911-X

David T. Johnson
Poverty, Inequality and Social Welfare in Australia
1996. ISBN 3-7908-0942-X

Rongxing Guo
Border-Regional Economics
1996. ISBN 3-7908-0943-8

Oliver Fratzscher
The Political Economy of Trade Integration
1996. ISBN 3-7908-0945-4

Ulrich Landwehr
Industrial Mobility and Public Policy
1996. ISBN 3-7908-0949-7

Arnold Picot/Ekkehard Schlicht (Eds.)
Firms, Markets, and Contracts
1996. Corr. 2nd printing 1997. ISBN 3-7908-0947-0

Thorsten Wichmann
Agricultural Technical Progress and the Development of a Dual Economy
1997. ISBN 3-7908-0960-8

Ulrich Woitek
Business Cycles
1997. ISBN 3-7908-0997-7

Michael Carlberg
International Economic Growth
1997. ISBN 3-7908-0995-0

Massimo Filippini
Elements of the Swiss Market for Electricity
1997. ISBN 3-7908-0996-9

Giuseppe Gaburro (Ed.)
Ethics and Economics
1997. ISBN 3-7908-0986-1

Frank Hoster/Heinz Welsch/ Christoph Böhringer
CO_2 Abatement and Economic Structural Change in the European Internal Market
1997. ISBN 3-7908-1020-7

Christian M. Hafner
Nonlinear Time Series Analysis with Applications to Foreign Exchange Rate Volatility
1997. ISBN 3-7908-1041-X

Sardar M.N. Islam
Mathematical Economics of Multi-Level Optimisation
1998. ISBN 3-7908-1050-9

Sven-Morten Mentzel
Real Exchange Rate Movements
1998. ISBN 3-7908-1081-9

Lei Delsen/Eelke de Jong (Eds.)
The German and Dutch Economies
1998. ISBN 3-7908-1064-9

Mark Weder
Business Cycle Models with Indeterminacy
1998. ISBN 3-7908-1078-9

Tor Rødseth (Ed.)
Models for Multispecies Management
1998. ISBN 3-7908-1001-0

Michael Carlberg
Intertemporal Macroeconomics
1998. ISBN 3-7908-1096-7

Sabine Spangenberg
The Institutionalised Transformation of the East German Economy
1998. ISBN 3-7908-1103-3

continued on page 129

Dirk Willer

The Development of Equity Capital Markets in Transition Economies

Privatisation and Shareholder Rights

With 5 Figures
and 26 Tables

Physica-Verlag
A Springer-Verlag Company

Series Editors
Werner A. Müller
Martina Bihn

Author
Dr. Dirk Willer
Centre of Economic Performance
London School for Economics
Houghton Street
London WC2A 2AE, United Kingdom

Cataloging-in-Publication Data applied for
Die Deutsche Bibliothek – CIP-Einheitsaufnahme
Willer, Dirk: The development of equity capital markets in transition economies: privatisation and shareholder rights; with 26 tables/Dirk Willer. – Heidelberg: Physica-Verl., 1999
(Contributions to economics)
ISBN-13: 978-3-7908-1198-8 e-ISBN-13: 978-3-642-99809-6
DOI: 10.1007/978-3-642-99809-6

Softcover Design: Erich Kirchner, Heidelberg

SPIN 10715966 88/2202-5 4 3 2 1 0 – Printed on acid-free paper

Acknowledgments

The transition of the formerly communist economies towards some form of capitalism is surely one of the main economic and political events of this decade. I consider it a great privilege to have been able to work on such a fascinating topic during the last years. I would very much like to thank my joint supervisors Richard Layard and David Webb for giving me the opportunity to do that. I am deeply indebted to Richard Layard for taking me to Russia. Working as part of his team I have benefited greatly from his insights into the Russian economy and politics. Furthermore, I am very grateful for Richard's remarkable generosity in providing a stimulating working environment at the Centre for Economic Performance. I am equally indebted to David Webb, who has been a great teacher of finance over the years. I was fortunate to work with him and his encouragement has been invaluable.

My research has been influenced by many discussions with my colleagues and friends which were in some way involved with the Russia effort of the LSE's Centre for Economic Performance and the Russian European Centre for Economic Policy (RECEP): In the first place I would like to thank Peter Boone with whom I have the pleasure to continue the collaboration in the private sector. I would also like to thank Alisdair Breach, Clemens Grafe, Liam Halligan, Rory MacFarquhar, Simon Johnson, Oleg Larichev, Yaroslav Lissovolik, Roland Nash, Peter Orszag, Sergei Prudnik, Andrea Richter, Kaspar Richter and Pavel Teplukhin, not least for their pleasant company. I am also grateful to Sergei Pavlenko, former Head of the government's Working Centre for Economic Reform, and Sergei Vasiliev, former Deputy Minister of the Economy, for being very supportive of my research.

I would also like to express my gratitude to Norbert Reetz for getting me interested in economics in the first place. Furthermore, I would like to thank Gilles Alfandari, Stephen Barber, Joseph Blasi, Dieter Boes, Markus Brunnermeier, Ulrike Burchardi, Leonardo Felli, Per Mellstroem, Jim Nail, Max Steuer, Anthony Richards, Kevin Roberts and seminar participants at the London School of Economics and the 1996 European Economic Association

Annual Conference for comments and suggestions.

Lastly, in many ways this dissertation would not have been possible without the constant encouragement and support of my parents, Helga and Erich to whom I would like to dedicate this book.

Financial support of the European Commission, the Studienstiftung des Deutschen Volkes and the ESRC is gratefully acknowledged.

Abstract

The book focuses on two issues that have arisen during the development of equity capital markets in transition economies. First, it has typically been observed that the divestiture of state assets in Russia has not been implemented comprehensively. Following an introductory chapter, the second chapter develops a model to explain this observation in an environment where the objective of the state is to maximize revenues from the sale of its shares on the equity capital markets. If the state has private information about the future macroeconomic environment or about potential improvements of the firms' qualities due to improved corporate governance it can signal its private information to investors. This can be achieved by choosing a percentage of the state's shareholdings to be held back from the immediate sales.

A second issue which has typically slowed down the development of capital equity markets in transition economies has been the violation of shareholder rights. Governments have often not guaranteed such rights. However, management might have incentives to introduce shareholder rights voluntarily. The third chapter develops a simple static framework to think about the issue of shareholder rights and tests some of its predictions. The chapter presents evidence from a sample of the 140 largest Russian joint stock companies. Only a minority of firms in this sample do honour shareholder rights and the chapter analyzes which firms are more likely to do that. It turns out that large firms are more likely to introduce shareholder rights, possibly because the expected value of stealing profits is smaller. Furthermore, there is some evidence that large outside blockholders as well as the state in its role as shareholder are able to press for shareholder rights.

The fourth chapter develops a dynamic model for the introduction of shareholder rights where the firm's ownership is endogenised. The chapter shows that in the short run, management might be willing to introduce shareholder rights only if it has received a sufficiently large portion of the firm's voting shares in the privatisation process. In the long term, more firms will introduce such rights, but only after they have stolen a sufficient part of the firms profits to build up a large equity stake.

Contents

1. Introduction 1
1.1 Partial Privatisation 2
1.2 Corporate Governance 12
1.3 The Structure of the Book 17

2. Why is Privatisation of Residual State-Owned Stakes Delayed ? 19
2.1 Introduction 19
2.2 The Model 24
2.2.1 Agents 24
2.2.2 Time Pattern 24
2.2.3 Firms 24
2.2.4 Information Structure 26
2.2.5 Strategies 26
2.2.6 Equilibrium Concept 28
2.3 Separating and Pooling Equilibria 29
2.4 Social Welfare 34
2.5 Conclusion 37
2.6 Appendix A 38
2.6.1 Proof of Proposition 2.1 38
2.6.2 Proof of Proposition 2.2 42
2.7 Appendix B 43

3. Shareholder Rights in Russia: An Empirical Investigation . 47
3.1 Introduction 47
3.2 Which Firms Honour Shareholder Rights ? A Simple Framework 50
3.2.1 Complete Management Control 50
3.2.2 Limited Management Control 53
3.2.3 Two Caveats 55
3.3 The Data 57
3.3.1 The Dependent Variables: Shareholder Rights Indicators 57
3.3.2 Independent Variables 63
3.4 Testing the Hypotheses 67

3.5 Conclusion 79
3.6 Appendix 81
3.6.1 The Index z_1 81
3.6.2 Additional Data and Regressions 82

4. Corporate Governance without State Guaranteed Shareholder Rights 87
4.1 Introduction 87
4.2 The Two Period Model 90
4.2.1 Management 91
4.2.2 Investors 94
4.2.3 Timing 95
4.2.4 Equilibrium Concept 95
4.2.5 Optimal Dividends 96
4.2.6 A Case where Shareholder Rights are Never Introduced 97
4.2.7 Two Cases where Shareholder Rights are Introduced .. 97
4.3 The Three Period Game 103
4.3.1 Allowing for Money-Laundering 104
4.3.2 Conditions for Introduction of Shareholder Rights 105
4.4 Social Welfare 108
4.5 Conclusion 109
4.6 Appendix A 113
4.7 Appendix B 113
4.7.1 Proof of Lemma 4.1 113
4.7.2 Proof of Proposition 4.1 114
4.7.3 Proof of Lemma 4.2 114
4.7.4 Proof of Lemma 4.3 115
4.7.5 Proof of Proposition 4.2 115
4.7.6 Proof of Lemma 4.4 116
4.7.7 Proof of Proposition 4.3 116
4.7.8 Proof of Proposition 4.4 117

List of Figures 119

List of Tables 121

Bibliography 123

1. Introduction

This book addresses two different but related topics that can arise during the development of equity capital markets and which could possibly hinder their development: partial privatisation and shareholder rights. Both issues are developed in the context of transition economies in general and Russia in particular. Chapter 2 puts forward a theory of partial privatisation, i.e. a model that aims to explain why the state keeps some residual shares. Several recent surveys for Russia have shown that the state does often not actively use the voting rights of its residual shares. If this was true, partial privatisation could entrench management and hinder restructuring. It would also limit the supply of shares, which could lead to low liquidity. This would be likely to slow down the development of the equity capital market. However, the model in chapter 2 shows that it can be rational to hold back shares from sale in order to maximise privatisation receipts. Another issue which holds back the development of this market is the fact that shareholder rights cannot be guaranteed by the state due to weak institutions. Chapter 3 contains an empirical examination of which firms honour shareholder rights and also provides a direct link between this problem and partial privatisation. Maybe surprisingly, some weak evidence is presented that shows that the residual state holding does not exert a negative influence with respect to the introduction of shareholder rights, but might even be a weak positive force. Chapter 4 proposes a mechanism, which could limit the problem of non-enforceable shareholder rights, but mostly only in the long run.

This introductory chapter aims to give some empirical background for the partial nature of the privatisation process in Russia and derives different hypotheses from the literature for why this might be observed. The following chapters do not aim to distinguish between the different hypotheses empirically, but instead add one more model to the list which also could explain partial privatisation. Several qualitative arguments are provided for why this particular model is one of the more plausible ones in the context of Russia. In a second step this introductory chapter puts forward different hypotheses from the literature on the optimal amount of management ownership with respect to efficient corporate governance. This book adds the case where management should be allocated a comparatively large stake. Chapter 4 illustrates why this would be the optimal privatisation policy in the context of the introduction of shareholder rights.

1.1 Partial Privatisation

Partial privatisation is defined as privatisation where the state keeps some remaining shares. Conceptually, a period where the state is a shareholder in a firm can be the outcome of two different strategies. First, it can be the desired outcome of the privatisation process that the state remains a shareholder. Second, partial state ownership can be a transition state when the desired outcome is complete privatisation. This is the case when the preferred sell-off process is a gradual one. A gradual sell-off process can consist of at least two, but possibly more auctions. Russia is one case where the sell-off process has been gradual so far. In the first stage of privatisation, lasting from 1992 to 1994, shares were auctioned off in exchange for so-called vouchers, which had been given for free to the population. In these auctions, on average, 30% of chartered capital was auctioned off. Another 50% was given away in closed auctions to insiders according to the most popular privatisation option. Vouchers stopped being traded by the end of the first stage of privatisation. These privatisation auctions were followed by the second stage of privatisation. On July 22 1994 President Yeltsin released a decree determining the basic concept of the second stage. According to this decree the remaining shares held by the state were to be divested through cash auctions and investment tenders, where the shares on offer were sold to the highest bidder. As will be shown below, these sell-offs were implemented, in general, not with one last auction, but often by several.

There are several data sources on residual state ownership in the case of Russia. Two early surveys of 1994 show the extent of the residual state ownership after the first stage of privatisation. First, according to a survey by the World Bank in mid 1994, 30% of firms in the sample were still state controlled (SO), and the mean state holding amounted to 89%. In worker controlled firms (WO) the mean stake was 10%; in manager controlled (MO) it was 13%; and in outsider controlled (OO) it was 12%. Overall, this implies a residual state ownership of 34%. The variance of the state stake was substantial.

Second, a survey of seven regional state property funds provides data for 1994 also. In 28.7% of cases the state still held more than 20% after the voucher privatisation had largely been concluded.

Clearly, a substantial remaining share ownership by the state was to be expected towards the end of the first stage of privatisation, given the mechanism used for privatisation. To assess the divestiture of the residual state stakes, more recent data provided by the Russian National Survey can be used. In this survey, a smaller sample of firms was analysed and a smaller average share ownership by the state is reported. Importantly, this survey

Table 1.1. World Bank Survey of 439 Industrial Firms, Mid-1994

State ownership	SO	WO	MO	OO	DN	Total
mean	89	10	13	12	1	34
std dev	21	14	15	13	5	40
% of firms	30	37	11	10	12	100

Source: Earle, Estrin, Leshchenko, 1996

Table 1.2. Survey of 7 Regional Property Funds, August 1994

Retained State Ownership	0	0.1-5	5.1-10	10.1-15	15.1-20	>20	Total
%	34.9	8.6	8.7	9.2	9.6	28.7	100.0

Source: Privatisation Project Regional Fund Survey, in Pistor and Turkewitz, 1994

indicates that the average ownership of the state was constant in 1995 but fell sharply in 1996. This indicates that the second stage of privatisation only gathered pace in 1996.

Table 1.3. The Russian National Survey

	1994	1995	1996
State ownership	13	13	9
Number of firms in survey	142	322	357

Source: Russian National Survey, in Blasi et al, 1997

More detailed information on state ownership reveals that in 1996 the median state ownership was 0% in the Russian National Survey (RNS) as well as in the data that will be presented for the largest traded firms in chapter 3. The state seemed to have held on to relatively large stakes in a small number of firms. It is also noteworthy, that the state held on average higher stakes in the largest traded firms than in the more representative Russian National Survey.

While this data shows the extent of the residual state ownership and the effect of the second stage of privatisation on the overall state ownership, this data is silent on how the residual stakes were being sold. Unfortunately, comprehensive data on the extent of sales in different firms is not available.

Table 1.4. State Ownership by Percentile

Percentile of State Ownership	5%	10%	25%	50%	75%	90%	95%
RNS, 1995	0	0	0	9	20	38	49
RNS, 1996	0	0	0	0	20	32	44
Large traded firms, 1996	0	0	0	0	20	40	51

Source: Russian National Survey, in Blasi et al, 1997

However, table 1.5 illustrates several auctions in which the state sold off only a fraction of its remaining stake in one given auction. This data is provided for the oil industry. The reason is that among the large firms, for which data is collected by financial firms, the oil industry has been the one for which the second stage of privatisation was implemented first.

In some cases listed in table 1.5, the state had not previously sold any shares in auctions to insiders or to the population. This was the case as some of the most valuable assets had been excluded from the general privatisation program. Furthermore, some of the firms are holding companies, created only after privatisation had already started. In this case it would have been the subsidiaries, of which shares had previously been sold in voucher auctions.

Outside the oil industry, there are some other examples of a partial privatisation strategy. For example, in Q3 1997 50% of Svjazinvest, the long distance communications firm, were sold off. The government has announced that another 25% is going to be sold during Q4 1998. *Perotti (1995)* provides some evidence of partial privatisation in the early stages of the Hungarian privatisation program.

The shares in auctions in the second stage were sold to blockholders. The presidential decree that initiated the second stage of privatisation explicitly states that one goal of that stage is to create blockholders who could play a positive role in corporate governance. This was achieved by allocating the full package of shares that was put up for sale to the highest bidder. The sample of *Blasi et al* presented in table 1.6 does show a slight increase in blockholdings. By early 1996 average blockholders held close to 30% in the *Blasi et al* sample as well as in the data presented in chapter 3. This is due to the second stage of privatisation as well as block-building on the secondary market.

For partial privatisation there have been several explanations proposed in the literature, mostly in the context of privatisation programmes in Western countries. First, there are two different hypotheses which would tend to result in a permanent state holding of some shares. In particular, it has been proposed, that the state only partially sells off firms in order to be able to

Table 1.5. Partial Privatisation in the Oil Industry

Name	Auction Date	% of shares sold	remaining state ownership
Sibneft	2-2-96	14.3	85.7
	1-9-96	15.0	70.7
	20-9-96	19.0	51.7
	30-12-98	0.7	51.0
	12-5-97	51.0	0.0
KomiTEK	21-1-97	38.0	51.0
	21-4-97	29.3	21.7
	19-9-97	20.6	1.1
Lukoil	7-12-95	5.0	27.0
	22-12-97	0.3	26.7
	planned for Q4 1998	6.0	20.7
VNK	8-12-97	50.0	35.0
	24-11-97	34.0	1.0
Slavneft	22-1-97	2.1	87.9
	14-11-97	2.1	85.8
	planned for 1998	19.7	66.1
TNK	18-6-97	40.0	51.0
	20-12-97	48.7	2.3
	16-3-98	0.1	2.2
Rosneft	30-3-98	75.0	25.0
	planned for Q4 1998	21.3	3.7

Source: Brunswick Warburg

Table 1.6. Blockholders in Russian Firms

	1994	1995	1996
Average holding of blockholder	11%	15%	16%
Companies with at least one blockholder	57%	71%	74%

Source: *Blasi et al, 1997*

keep some influence over the firms. There are several hypotheses linked to this argument, depending on the underlying assumption on the objective function of the state. First, *Boes (1991)* assumes that the state maximises social welfare while private owners maximise profits, denoted by Π. The compromise between private and public shareholders takes place at the level of the board and the bargaining power depends on the extent of the residual shareholding of the state, denoted by Θ. The objective of the partially privatised firm therefore is to choose a price p for its output which maximises

$$\Phi = \Theta[S(p) + \Pi(p)] + (1 - \Theta)\Pi(p) \tag{1.1}$$

where S denotes the consumer surplus. A 100% private firm maximises only profits, while a 100% public firm maximises only welfare. A privatised firm with some remaining public share-ownership maximises a weighted average of the two. On the other hand, *Boes* assumes that the larger the extent of privatisation (i.e. the smaller Θ) the further is the production possibility frontier shifted outwards. This implies that in general an optimal $\Theta > 0$ is found in cases when the firm is active in less than fully competitive markets. Under perfect competition profit maximization implies maximization of welfare at the same time. This limits this theory to some extent. A second limitation is the implicit assumption that a private firm will be allowed to maximise profits even in a monopolistic market. However, this freedom is in general restricted by regulation. *Boes* consequently adapts his model by introducing asymmetric information. In particular, he assumes that the state as a shareholder learns about shocks to demand as well as about shocks to costs. The state as a regulator, on the other hand, only knows about the distributions of such shocks. The author can then show that partial privatisation is, under certain restrictions, still the optimal outcome of the privatisation process, as regulation under incomplete information faces severe problems.

HYPOTHESIS 1a (*Boes*, 1991): The observation of the state holding on to a residual package of shares can be explained by its improved access to information and increased influence on the management's decision due to its representation on the board of directors. This improved information allows the state to maximise a weighted average of welfare and profits, as opposed to only profits, in industries that are less than fully competitive.

However, the assumption of the state as a benevolent dictator is a strong one. In particular, in transition economies one principal reason for privatisation has been that the state was thought to have objectives other than profit maximization, such as employment, which could be detrimental to restructuring [1]. Such objectives could result in inefficiencies and underperformance (see, for example, *Estrin and Perotin, 1991*). *Boycko et al (1992)* as well as *Shleifer and Vishny (1994)* argue that governments will find it harder to induce privatised firms to non profit-maximising behaviour, because government might have to 'bribe' management with money raised through distortionary taxation to implement certain policies. As in the setting of *Boes*, these arguments have to be placed in a setting of asymmetric information, as otherwise regulation could be used to fulfil the state's objectives. *Hart (1995)* also stresses that even in the presence of agency costs, differences in asset ownership do not matter as long as contracts are complete. Privatisation in the context of asymmetric information is, for example, modelled by *Schmidt (1996)*, who argues that the crucial difference between privatised and state-owned firms is that the government has less information about the firm if it does not also own it. If management has information superior to that of government it can be harder for the government to fulfil its other objectives. This, in turn, can increase the efficiency of privatised firms. To the extent that partial state ownership allows the state to keep receiving information on the firm, this could also explain residual share ownership by the state.

HYPOTHESIS 1b (based on *Schmidt*, 1996): The observation of the state holding on to a residual package of shares can be explained by its improved access to information due to it being able to put directors on the board. This improved information allows the state to implement its objectives other than profit maximization, such as securing a certain level of employment.

Estrin (1994) is more concerned with (ex ante) political constraints. He points out that distributing the shares to the general population does not take into account the interests of management and workers, who can potentially derail the privatisation process. For example, with enterprise managers well represented in the Russian parliament, a privatisation law favouring outside investors might never have been passed. In the context of partial privatisation, it can be argued that insiders were willing to allow for privatisation of some percentage of a given firm, but prevented the full sale. This could be a possibility, as the residual state ownership could have been thought to prevent a hostile take-over, at least in case managers expected that the state would not use the votes attached to its shares.

[1] Furthermore, the literature on political economy illustrates that the objectives of politicians who maximise their election results do in general differ from those of a benevolent dictator.

HYPOTHESIS 2 (based on *Estrin*, 1994): The observation of the state holding on to a residual package of shares can be explained by political constraints, which did not allow for the complete sell-off of the firms.

In case the state is concerned about the revenues of privatisation the following four hypotheses have been proposed:

HYPOTHESIS 3a (based on *Demougin and Sinn, 1992*): The observation of the state holding on to a residual package of shares can be explained by its objective of minimising the costs of privatisation due to insufficient liquidity for a complete sell-off.

This hypothesis assumes that there is only a limited amount of capital that could be used to buy the shares, i.e., that investors are credit constrained. If the pool of capital is restricted, prices would clearly have to be lower for a large issue than for a small one. Such an argument seems mainly applicable to an economy which is closed with respect to capital flows.

A similar argument has been put forward by *Jenkinson and Mayer* (1994), who argue that a disposal of assets in stages is the best strategy to avoid mispricing. While in the first auctions for many British privatisations underpricing was substantial, this effect decreased in subsequent auctions.

HYPOTHESIS 3a (*Jenkinson and Mayer*, 1994): The observation of the state holding on to a residual package of shares can be explained by its objective of minimising the costs of privatisation due to the mispricing of shares.

This argument implicitly assumes that the market-price that results in the secondary market the day after the initial privatisation auction, is closer to the fundamental value of the assets than the price set by the state for the privatisation auction. If the state had better information, the difference between issue price and market price would not necessarily be a cost of the privatisation process. The assumption that the market has superior information might be justified since the price in the capital market aggregates the information of all the participants in the trading process. This argument is related to *Dewatripont and Roland (1993)*, who make a point on the timing of reforms in general, incorporating imperfect knowledge about optimal reforms on the side of policy makers. The main ingredient is that policy makers are learning about which reforms are optimal and/or how to implement them. The price set for the initial tenders could be interpreted as one issue about which policy makers will learn over time. Their model would also imply that the sell-off of state shares should be gradual. However, one question raised by these arguments is why the state does not immediately use a tender to avoid mispricing. Such tenders would result in a situation where the price in the initial auction is already the market price. If such mechanisms were employed, there could still be some underpricing, if investors are risk-averse and are less willing to bid if the outcome is highly uncertain. However, the marginal investor could be risk-neutral and in this case this would not apply. Moreover, the assumptions about the distribution of information in the above argument are rather strong. In the case of initial public offerings (IPO) of firms, it is assumed by most of the literature that the seller, i.e. the entrepreneur, has inside knowledge, whereas the market is at an informational disadvantage. Chapter 2 of this book provides a model which retains the assumption of a revenue maximising state, but assumes that the state as a seller has private information. Under these assumptions it is shown that the state can signal the quality of the firms (and the future macroeconomic environment) by retaining some shares in the firms to be privatised.

HYPOTHESIS 4 (chapter 2): The observation of the state holding on to a residual package of shares can be explained by its objective to maximise revenues and its ability to do that by signalling inside information on the value of the assets by a strategic choice of the amount of shares to be sold off.

The model is related to models of IPOs and in particular to *Leland and Pyle (1977)*. One key difference is that the value of the firm in the model of chapter 2 depends on how much is sold off, whereas *Leland and Pyle* have to rely on a risk-averse entrepreneur whose utility rises the more is sold off due to improved diversification. Furthermore, *Allan and Faulhaber* (1989) propose a model where the firm has inside information. In their model firms can use underpricing in the initial share issue as a signal that the firm being sold is of high quality. Bad firms cannot copy the behaviour of good firms, because only good firms can underprice and nevertheless pay a high dividend in the next period. Subsequently, further equity is sold off and the price in the second issue depends on whether a firm was able to signal its high quality in the initial issue or not. Clearly, such a strategy only makes sense in the case of partial privatisation, as otherwise there would be no subsequent share-issue where the state could be rewarded for selling at a discount in the initial auction. However, for the case of a privatisation, a price signal as in the *Allan and Faulhaber* model is not possible. The high quality firm which is privatised is not able to signal its quality by artificially lowering its proceeds in the initial auction and paying dividends nevertheless, because the *state* obtains the revenues from the initial auction. Therefore, the proceeds from the first auction have no impact whatsoever on the financial situation of the firm.

HYPOTHESIS 5 (*Perotti, 1995*): The observation of the state holding on to a residual package of shares can be explained by its objective to maximise revenues and its intention to demonstrate to market participants that it will refrain from expropriating shareholders.

Only if it is believed that the government is not going to expropriate shareholders will management operate efficiently and will investors attach a high valuation to the assets. One problem with this set-up is that it assumes that the policy maker does not change. In case political changes were expected the market price would not depend on whether the present government would be of an expropriating type or of a non-expropriating type.

It is difficult to distinguish between the different hypotheses and this book does not attempt to do this empirically. However, there are several arguments which - for the case of Russia - make hypothesis 4 more likely than rival hypotheses. First, it has to be realised that there is a very basic difference between the privatisation processes one would observe according to hypotheses 1 and 2 on the one hand and hypotheses 3 to 5 on the other hand. Both of the former hypotheses would argue for a privatisation process that is *and remains* partial, as the benefits which the state obtains from its holdings are in general constant over time. With respect to hypothesis 2 this is true unless the political environment would have changed in a way that allows further privatisation. Hypotheses 3 to 5, on the contrary, would imply that the observation of residual state ownership would be a temporary phenomenon and that the final outcome of the privatisation process would be 100% private firms. For the oil industry, table 1.5 shows that the state has sold off its total residual holdings in some firms, providing some evidence in support of hypothesis 3 to 5. However, in other industries residual holdings remain. As underlined by the objective of the Russian Ministry of Finance to collect about USD4bn in privatisation revenues for the federal budget during 1998, the privatisation process in Russia is not yet finished. In the absence of facts on the final sell-off patterns, only statements of government plans can be analysed. And indeed, according to the presidential decree on the second stage of privatisation the aim seems to be to transfer 100% of stakes into private hands apart from several 'strategic enterprises', which are going to remain state owned and are mostly in the defence industry, but also include some monopolies in other industries. This also would tend to provide some support for hypothesis 3 to 5. The privatisation plans seem to be driven by severe fiscal imbalances, which are typical in the first years of transition. In this situation, the generation of budget revenues has been of high importance to policy makers. This is in particular the case, as it has turned out to be very difficult to raise sufficient taxes in some of the transition economies (in particular in the FSU) since the countries are plagued by a comparatively large shadow economy. At the same time, taxation is rather costly in these economies as high tax rates on the official sector of the economy lead to large distortions in that sector. For example, high taxation is one of the reasons why more and more Russian firms use barter to escape taxation (see, for example *Russian Economic Barometer*). Given that it is, in general, the case that government debt markets are not very well developed in the initial phase of reforms, privatisation is seen as an important way to solve fiscal problems. Of course, privatisation only matters in this context if capital markets are imperfect or if there are gains in efficiency (i.e. if the firms become more valuable under private ownership). Otherwise, the state could borrow against future income from its state-owned firms, which would alleviate its fiscal constraint in exactly the same way as an outright sale. This line of argument, centering on a fiscal story can also be fitted to the initial privatisation program in

Hungary, which was saddled with a very large stock of foreign debt. However, due to the perceived slowness of the privatisation efforts in Hungary the government changed tack and proceeded to sell off a larger extent to insiders than had previously been planned.

The other argument against hypothesis one, for the case of Russia, would be that partial privatisation has been the observed outcome in many firms which operate in industries where conditions are close to competitive, and the state is therefore unlikely to hold further shares in order to improve social welfare. The same argument can be used against the proposition of *Perotti*, as the state can most easily expropriate shareholders in regulated industries. Many Russian privatised firms are not regulated by the state in any meaningful way.

The argument against hypothesis 1b) is slightly more difficult to make, as it relies on the unobservable attitude of government towards privatisation. If the government wanted for exogenous (maybe political) reasons to keep maximising employment as opposed to profits, it would be keen to keep a director on the board in order to obtain sufficient information to allow it to do so. However, this would go very much against the grain of the privatisation process and the initial impetus behind it. Accounts of the privatisation process so far stress how the process was pushed through in order to de-politicise the firms *(Boycko et al, 1992)*. In this situation it seems unlikely that the privatisation process was implemented only partially in order to prevent a full depolitisation. However, it might have been the case that the state subsequently discovered that its voting rights attached to the shares could help it to push for other objectives on the reformist agenda. In particular, chapter 3 presents some weak evidence, that the state as a shareholder might be able to increase the likelihood that shareholder rights are honoured. To the extent that the mechanism that is proposed in chapter 4 to overcome the problem of insufficient shareholder rights is second best, the state can raise welfare by pushing for shareholder rights.

The validity of hypothesis 2 is difficult to assess empirically. While there was significant evidence of ex-ante political constraints on the privatisation process, which had to be passed by the communist dominated Russian parliament, there is less direct evidence that management can prevent the sell-off of the residual shares the state still holds. However, the absence of this direct evidence does not mean that hypothesis 2 does not explain some of the residual state holdings.

Hypothesis 3a is unlikely to hold for Russia. *Boycko et al (1992)* have been arguing that lack of liquidity has not been the case during privatisation in Russia as foreign participation was in principal possible and Russia was characterised by very large capital outflows. In case domestic investors would have perceived shares in privatisation auctions to be underpriced due to a lack of liquidity (and not to be priced correctly at very low levels because of the high risk involved in these firms) this capital could have been used in the privatisation process. Also, there were no restrictions for Russian banks to borrow abroad. Such borrowing could have been securitised with the shares to be acquired. In particular, if the shares were perceived to be sold at undervalued prices due to liquidity constraints Western banks would have found it in their interest to provide such loans. However, illiquidity in the absence of tight legal restrictions preventing any international capital flows is interpreted by *Glosten and Milgrom (1985)* as being due to asymmetric information. Illiquidity implies that prices fall to a large extent when a given amount of shares is sold. *Glosten and Milgrom* argue that this is the case as buyers suspect that the seller has inside information. This is exactly the mechanism underlying hypothesis 4 and allows the state to signal its inside information.

Hypothesis 3b is unlikely to hold for the case of Russia, as many of the firms had already been privatised in the first stage of privatisation. Following this stage, a market for shares had developed (taking over from the relatively liquid voucher market) and a market price was therefore already available. However, for some individual cases of privatisation this line of argument might well be relevant. For example, 51% of the telecom holding company Svjazinvest was sold off in late 1997, which is going to be followed by two more auctions for 25% in Q4 1998 and 1999. For this firm, there had been no initial voucher privatisation which led to some uncertainty with respect to the appropriate price in the initial auction. However, this uncertainty was mitigated as many of the subsidiaries of Svjazinvest had been traded before the initial auction. The same is true for some of the oil companies, most notably Rosneft. As pointed out above, hypothesis 3 also relies on the assumption that the state has no inside information *vis-a-vis* the (potentially foreign) buyer. This does not seem plausible, at least not for every firm.

With respect to hypothesis 5 it has to be realised that one basic characteristic of Russia has been the almost constant threat of a reversal on the political side. This is demonstrated by the victories of the Communists in the 1995 parliamentary election as well as the 1996 regional elections. In addition, there was a highly uncertain presidential election in 1996 and several health scares with respect to President Yeltsin between 1996 and 1998. This would undermine one of the most important assumptions of *Perotti* and makes it unlikely that investors are willing to pay higher prices based on the characteristics of the present government. All these factors underline the relevance of hypothesis 4 for the case of Russia. The underlying model for this hypothesis is developed in chapter 2.

1.2 Corporate Governance

The question of corporate governance is closely connected with privatisation. The outcome of privatisation in terms of ownership structure is a key determinant for how well the corporate governance system works. However, an efficient system of corporate governance is also closely linked to another aspect of transition: the building of institutions. Whether institutions like a bankruptcy procedure or shareholder rights are implemented by governments does affect the functioning of corporate governance. However, to some extent firms can introduce such rights even in the absence of state guarantees.

One of the most important issues with respect to corporate governance, in particular for transition economies, is the issue of ability versus incentives of management. From a theoretical point of view, a system of corporate governance has to be constructed which facilitates that the most able person is allocated the job of manager and that his incentives are optimal. However, those two objectives are not necessarily consistent with each other. Assuming that the productivity of the firm depends both on the manager's ability as well as on costly efforts by the manager, there is a moral hazard problem. In a standard principal agent setting, the cost of the manager of generating a profit π is denoted by $C(\pi, t)$, where t represents the ability of the manager. The principal does not know t, but knows the distribution from which it is drawn. An extreme example for the costs of management to increase profits could be that he stops to expropriate shareholders by stealing. To induce some effort from management, the principal must offer a compensation schedule that depends on profits, for example in a linear form: $s + r\pi$, where s and r are constants. As management maximises his payoff, it sets optimally

$$\frac{\partial C(\pi, t)}{\partial \pi} = r \tag{1.2}$$

Managerial effort is set efficiently in case $r = 1$. However, such a payment scheme might induce short-term profit maximization, possibly by running down the assets of the firm *(Holmstroem, 1982)*. Therefore, the payment must be linked to future profits as well. *McMillan (1995)* observes that this is done in Western countries by stock options, which are in general not available in transition economies due to the rudimentary state of the stock markets. *McMillan* points out that a possible solution of this incentive problem is to give management shares. *Pinto et al (1993)* report evidence for Poland where state-firm managers motivation was long run as they expected that they would acquire shares at low prices when the firms were eventually privatised. But clearly, if r is interpreted as the percentage of shares given to management, the higher r, the less likely is it that management with a low ability can be removed, at least if there are significant private benefits from controlling the firm such that management is not easily bribed out of its job. Due to this trade-off it is *a priori* not clear how policy makers should structure the corporate governance system[2].

[2] In this context preference shares, i.e. shares without voting rights, could in general improve efficiency.

HYPOTHESIS 6 (*McMillan, 1995*): In general management should hold a positive stake in the firm, but less than 100%; $0 \leq r \leq 1$.

For transition economies there is a presumption that pre-privatisation management is often of low ability, as the skills needed under the state-planned economy were very different from the ones required in a market environment. Empirically, ***Barberis et al (1995)*** present some evidence from Russian privatised retail shops that restructuring was not significantly correlated with management's incentive schemes, but strongly with new management. *Johnson and Loveman (1995)* obtain similar conclusions from Polish case studies. Such findings would tend to imply that the firm should optimally be sold off to outsiders, preferably using auctions. In case there are no large differences in private benefits of control among different bidders, such auctions would tend to result in the investor winning the auction which can install the most able management[3]. To the extent that the expected ability is higher for management that is installed after an auction than for incumbent management, this new management should then receive more high-powered incentives than would be optimal for incumbent management: $\bar{r} \geq r$.

HYPOTHESIS 7 (based on *Feldman and Mehra, 1993*): Firms should be sold by auction, which increases the likelihood that the most able bidder is going to run the firm. Given that the expected ability of the auction's winner is in general higher than the expected ability of the incumbent management, the winning management should get more high powered incentives (ownership) than incumbent management: $\bar{r} \geq r$

It has been argued that benefits of sales to outsiders in an environment of weak legal institutions should take the form of block sales. For Russia, chapter 3 presents some evidence that shareholder rights are not easily enforceable. The variability of the index for shareholder rights indicates that many firms do not honour shareholder rights, presumably due to weak legal institutions. *Bergloef (1995)* hypothesises that in such an environment control-oriented finance (i.e. investors with concentrated equity or debt holdings, which do intervene actively in the firm's investment policies) is superior to arms-length finance (holding a diversified portfolio without direct interference) as it relies less on a well defined legal system. His hypothesis is given some credence by *La Porta et al (1996)*. They find that in countries with weak legal systems, equity and debt holdings are typically very concentrated. Chapter 3 gives some evidence that large outside blockholders do seem to have some power to press for the introduction of shareholder rights. Similarly, *Blasi and Shleifer (1996)* report that the likelihood of outside board representation increases with the size of the outside share ownership. However, this policy prescription seemed difficult to implement due to political pressure. In particular, there were formidable ex-ante political constraints

---

[3] *Cornelli and Lee (1995)* have shown that auctions should take on a more complicated form in case private benefits are likely to differ significantly.

against outsider privatisation (see *Boycko et al, 1995)*. The Russian parliament, largely dominated by the Communist Party, managed to prevent such a privatisation programme. Furthermore, management seems to try to prevent sales of shares to outsiders. One of the main buyers of shares sold by workers has been management. The ownership resulting in the Russian case is described in most detail by *Blasi et al (1997)*. In their sample of small and medium sized firms, insiders owned 58% of shares in 1996, down from 65% in 1994. Top management held 10%, up from 7% directly after the privatisation in 1994. In a separate question, management professed on average to aim for ownership of 50%. In 1996 employees were majority owners in 65% of firms. These figures underline the high extent of inside ownership. Employees have sold some of their shares to outsiders, but about half of their shares were sold to management. Management apparently could not prevent sales to outsiders completely, but managed to slow the process down. However, these developments were mainly recorded between 1994 and 1995. In 1996 the stake of insiders even rose slightly. From the theoretical point of view, management would have tried to block the sales of shares to workers in the same way as it blocked sales to outsiders if it had believed that it could not prevent workers from selling their shares to outsiders. Indeed, there is some evidence that management succeeded in preventing workers from selling out their shares. *Frydman et al (1996)* find in a survey of voucher funds, that management coerced workers into not selling and also, that workers would frequently be unwilling to sell. They believe that the latter might be true as workers are aiming to keep the firm insider dominated in order to keep their jobs. Furthermore, they point out that Russian voucher funds, one of the most important outside shareholders in the direct aftermath of privatisation, were regulated such that they would focus on the trading of securities, rather than on taking large stakes in individual firms. In particular, funds were limited to acquire no more than 10% in a single firm[4]. *Filatotchev et al (1995)* report that many companies require that the buyer and seller of a share need to attend the company's registered office in order to transfer shares. Furthermore, some company charters include the requirement to offer shares to management first. *Shleifer and Vasiliev (1996)* report that managers were also employing formal trust agreements to prevent workers from selling to outsiders. Such behaviour resulted in insider ownership being preserved for longer than had initially been hoped. Nevertheless, blockholder (defined as holding more than 5% of charter capital) existed in 57% of firms surveyed by *Blasi et al.* During the second stage of privatisation, shares were allocated to one winner of the auction, whereas the voucher auction resulted in much more disbursed share-ownership, as every person who entered his voucher into the auction received a corresponding allocation of shares. The distribution of shares to insiders also resulted in disbursed ownership, as the bulk of the shares were in general allocated to workers. Therefore, the second stage

[4] However, it turned out that this particular restriction was never enforced.

of privatisation helped to increase the number of blockholders in the Russian firms, in spite of difficulties in creating blocks by purchases in the secondary market. Data for the increase in the average holding of the blockholder as well as in the rise in the share of companies with at least one blockholder has been presented above.

Secondly, even if outside shareholders managed to build up a significant stake in a firm, there is some evidence that their control over management remains limited. In particular, the variability of the index of shareholder rights indicates that many firms do not honour shareholder rights, in spite of the existence of outside blockholders. While chapter 3 provides some evidence that an increase in the size of the largest blockholder increases the likelihood of shareholder rights being introduced, there is some evidence that even large blockholders can have severe difficulties in controlling management. *Blasi et al (1997)* report that in 1994 outsiders were in general denied to place directors on the board, although they owned on average 21% of the firm in their sample. Only in a few cases did outsiders and insiders find a compromise, which resulted in some outside representation on the boards. This left the large majority of firms in the control of management. From 1995 the representation of outsiders rose. This was mainly achieved not through open voting in shareholder meetings, but through private deals between management and some outsiders. In 1996, 31% of seats were held by outsiders. However, this figure is likely to overstate the true extent of outside influence, as management controlled firms are counted as outsiders. Also, it is likely that outsiders more easily gain representation in firms which are less valuable (where more restructuring is necessary), as insiders fight less in order to keep these assets under their control. In any case, even a board representation of 31% is not enough to exert control against the 69% held by management and the state, in particular, as the state until 1996 in general voted in line with managements' proposals. This would still leave the majority of Russia's valuable firms in the control of management. Similarly, *Blasi et al (1997)* report that of the 30% of firms that had exchanged their directors between 1992 and 1996, 80% of the replacements were from within the company. Furthermore, as late as 1996 60% of managers were opposed to making financial data available to outside investors[5]. *Boycko et al (1995)* report that some managers physically threaten challengers at shareholder meetings, rig shareholder votes or illegally change corporate charters. More generally, *Boone and Fedorov (1997)* report for the case of Russia, a widespread disregard for the law at every level of decision making. Given this evidence a model is developed in chapter

[5] A good example of how management cannot easily be made accountable to outside shareholders is the case of Komineft, where management in 1994 diluted outside shareholders in an apparently illegal manner. This violation could not be rectified by a court as laws were unclear and the local administration was on the side of management.

4 in which incumbent management cannot be replaced and therefore, ability is not modelled. In particular, the model focuses on investment decisions and shareholder rights in relation to management ownership.

HYPOTHESIS 8 (based on Chapter 4): To the extent that institutional weaknesses make it impossible (or very costly) to replace incumbent management, the trade-off between ability and incentives collapses and management should be given further increased ownership $\bar{\bar{r}} > \bar{r}$. Institutional weaknesses can to some extent be mitigated by management behaviour.

It is noteworthy, that in the context of chapter 4 preference shares for management would not increase efficiency since there is no mechanism to replace management, even in cases where management does not hold any voting rights.

Empirically, *Earle, Estrin and Leshchenko (1996)* do not find that differences in ownership translate in different strategies when it comes to restructuring. Similarly, changes in sales cannot be explained by differences in ownership. Capacity utilisation is similar among firms with dominant worker ownership, management ownership and state ownership. Lastly, when abstracting from de-novo firms, they do not find an impact of ownership on changes in employment. *Blasi et al (1997)* report that worker dominated firms did in general not pay higher wages or offer better social benefits to its workers. *Blasi et al (1997)* report that firms with outside directors on the board are more likely to restructure, but the evidence is not very strong and holds only for some measures of restructuring. Changing the director does not seem to matter for most indicators of restructuring; maybe that is the case because in 80% of such cases directors were replaced by insiders. The percentage of outside ownership and the amount of outside blockholding also does not have any influence on restructuring in the *Blasi et al (1997)* sample. However, *Earle and Estrin (1996)* find that privatised firms are more likely to restructure and tend to have higher productivity. Furthermore, they find that it is in particular management ownership which spurs increases in productivity as well as long term restructuring, measured by the correlation between the products sold before and after the introduction of reforms. This seems to give some limited empirical foundation for hypothesis 8.

1.3 The Structure of the Book

Chapter 2 develops the model on which hypothesis 4 of this introduction is based. It adds one more plausible theoretical explanation for the partial nature of privatisation in Russia. Chapter 4 puts forward the theoretical model on which hypothesis 8 of this introduction is based. It provides a theoretical argument for distributing a comparatively large amount of shares to management of privatized firms. This is done in the context of an analysis of the introduction of shareholder rights. The model is a dynamic one where management builds up stakes in firms over time. Only once management has built up sufficiently large stakes are shareholder rights introduced. Chapter 3 provides an initial empirical look at the question of the introduction of shareholder rights and sets the stage for chapter 4. The model is a static one and is to some extent a stripped-down version of the fuller model developed in chapter 4. It is nevertheless useful for an initial empirical analysis. First, given the data available it is not possible to test the dynamic model of chapter 4. In particular, data on insider ownership, which is the driving force of model 4, is not available. Furthermore, I have only data at one point in time, which makes it ill-suited for testing a dynamic model. Second, the data of early 1996 should provide very much an initial look on the issue of shareholder rights, given that the second stage of privatisation is still on-going in 1998. A static model therefore seems appropriate for the early 1996 data.

2. Why is Privatisation of Residual State-Owned Stakes Delayed ?

2.1 Introduction

There is a considerable variation across transition economies with respect to the implementation of privatisation programs. In Russia privatisation is comparatively far advanced. At the end of 1995, about 80% of the industrial enterprises (measured by employment) had been 'privatised'. However, the label 'privatised' does not mean that the state has transferred all shares in these companies to private agents. On the contrary, a World Bank Survey carried out in the summer of 1994, found that only in 35% of 'privatised' Russian firms the state held no shares. In 17% of firms the state ownership was between 0% and 10%, and in 19% of firms between 10% and 20%. In Hungary, the state still held shares in 34% of large firms, in 23% of which the state holding was below 50% *(Pistor and Turkewitz, 1994)*. However, this was partly a result of the fact that the privatisation in Russia happened in two stages. In the first stage, shares were allocated to insiders and sold in voucher auctions to the population. This phase ended in 1994. The residual share-ownership reported by *Pistor and Turkewitz* are the ones at the end of the first stage of privatisation. During the second stage of privatisation, which was introduced by a presidential decree in July 1994, shares were sold off for cash in auctions or investment tenders to blockholders.

This chapter is concerned with the second stage of privatisation. In this sense privatisation can be a misnomer for some firms. In case more than 50% of charter capital has been sold in the first stage of privatisation, the firm was already privatised and the auctions in the second stage are more precisely referred to as a divestiture of residual shares held by the state. Only in case less than 50% had been sold off in the first stage (which is true only for a minority of the Russian firms) the second stage of privatisation is a privatisation in the precise sense of the word. However, given that the term 'privatisation' is in general use also for the second stage, I shall stick to this term throughout this chapter.

In the auctions of the second stage it can be observed that the state did not always sell-off its complete residual holdings in one single auction, but sold only a fraction thereof, as has been shown for the case of the oil industry by the data reported in the introduction. These findings raise two

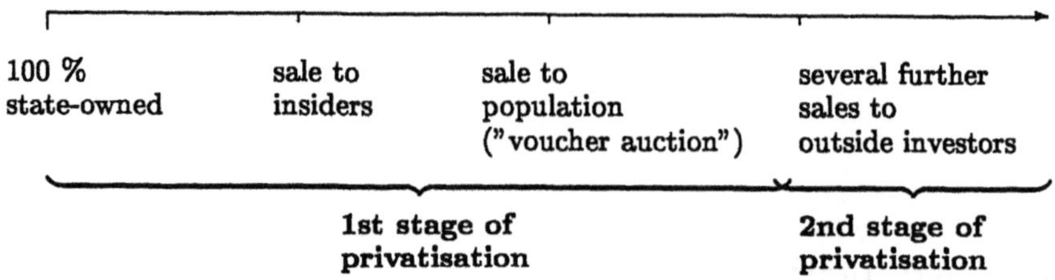

Fig. 2.1. Sequential Privatisation

questions: Why did the state not sell everything, given the prior commitment to privatisation ? And secondly, how can the variation in the withheld stakes be explained ?

The answer to the first question is given using a signalling framework: A model is constructed where the state has private information about the future macro-state of the economy. Its objective is to maximize proceeds from privatisation. The stakes the state keeps in the firms can then serve as signals. The larger the retained stakes, the more likely is a good macro-state in the future. These signals can be credible because they are costly. Assuming that the sale of a block of shares to a private investor improves corporate governance and therefore the value of these firms, the state pays a price when holding on to some shares. In this context it should be noted that during the first stage of privatisation, shares were largely sold to dispersed owners (workers and the population). Only in the second stage were shares sold to blockholders which were better positioned to improve corporate governance. On the other hand, signalling a good future macro-state increases the price investors are willing to pay for the shares sold today. A revenue maximizing state then might find it rational not to sell off 100% of its stakes. With different corporate governance gains for different firms the model can also explain why different degrees of privatisation are observed. If the potential corporate governance gains for a given firm are large, the state has a larger incentive to sell the firms today to realize these gains. Therefore, it is likely to sell more of firms with large potential corporate governance gains.

There exists an extensive literature on the sequencing of reforms, and in particular on the sequencing of privatisation. Most papers have so far focused either on the efficient allocation of resources or on political economy considerations (e.g., *Roland, 1994* or *Boycko et* al, 1992). However, in the recent past, the revenue generating function of privatisation seems to have become more important. This was mainly driven by the severe difficulties the federal government encountered in financing its deficit. Up to and including 1994, the government was still relying on direct credits from the Central Bank of Russia. This changed after the initiation of the IMF program in 1995. In 1995 about 50% of the federal budget deficit of 6% of GDP was financed by the sale of domestic debt at an average real interest rate of more than 150%. Such rates led to a very quick build up of the stock of federal domestic debt, which reached 19% of GDP at the end of 1996 - from close to 0% at the beginning of reform in 1992. In this situation revenues from privatisation were seen as a potentially very important source of revenue. The prime importance of this objective of privatisation was explicitly mentioned in a presidential decree of July 22 1994, which laid out the basic concept for the so called second stage of privatisation. That the importance of maximizing revenues (as opposed to letting the firms use the money for investment) was rising over time becomes apparent from two further presidential decrees. On May 11 1995 President Yeltsin signed a decree which altered the shares different institutions received from privatisation revenues. Not surprisingly, the share intended for the federal budget increased substantially from 10% of revenues to 35%. A further presidential decree of September 18 1996 raised the share of privatisation revenues that goes to the federal budget to 71%. This happened mainly at the expense of the share of the actual enterprise to be privatised, which previously had received 14% of revenues, but which would from then on not receive any money from the sale. The local budgets also saw their share cut. Lastly, the fact that enterprises were sold in auctions to the highest bidders, and not at a pre-set price as had been the case in some of the British privatisations, would also imply that revenues were maximized.

If one accepts that the government has indeed been trying to maximize revenues, there is still the question to be answered why this should be the case ? After all, citizens are presumably indifferent between the state giving firms away for free to the population and higher taxation on the one hand and selling the firms at high prices and correspondingly lower taxation. This would in particular seem to be the case as the use of voucher auctions would eliminate potentially unwarranted distributional consequences of a sale. However, this argument would tend to ignore two things. First, there is a real efficiency gain from allocating large shareholdings to blockholders as opposed to giving them away to the population. While these blockholders could then subsequently be taxed instead of acquiring shares at a high price, management might well try to hide any profits which makes subsequent taxation difficult. Therefore, not maximizing revenues would lead to unwarranted distributional consequences, i.e. a transfer from tax payers to the blockholder who obtains the shares. Second, maximizing revenues is in general an efficient mechanism to allocate the firms to the bidder who can use the assets most efficiently, at least when there are no significant differences in private benefits between different bidders (for an exception see *Cornelli and Lee, 1995*). If the state was not maximizing revenues and would as a result allocate the shares to an inefficient buyer, social welfare would be lower as well. Lastly, taxation induces inefficiencies, unless lump-sum taxes can be implemented. One standard result of public sector economics shows that taxing consumption leads to a deadweight loss the size of which is proportional to the tax rate to the power of two. This implies that increasing tax rates further raises the welfare costs substantially. If the alternative to privatisation revenues was taxation of personal income, distortionary effects are also likely to be significant. In a study by *Hausman (1981)*, it is shown that the US federal taxes at 1988 rates reduced labour supply by about 6.5%. Furthermore, the deadweight loss from all taxes on labour for the average married man were 13.5% of revenues raised by these taxes. These distortions are likely to be even more important in transition economies. Indirect evidence for this point comes from several sources: first, the mere size of the shadow economy implies that tax rates for the formal economy have to be relatively high (as expenditures are distributed in general to the whole economy, but revenues are only raised from the formal economy). Given that the cost of taxation increases rapidly in line with higher tax rates, increasing tax rates would be especially distortionary in an economy like Russia. Secondly, the fact that the government is apparently finding it difficult to raise taxes, largely because of tax avoidance, would also tend to underline that taxation must be comparatively distortionary in Russia. The difficulties in raising taxes are demonstrated by the fact that Russia has collected only 32% of GDP in general government revenues in 1996, of which it is thought that less than 60% was collected in cash. It is underlined further by the fact that the IMF has delayed several tranches of its loan to the Russian government, citing as the main reason that the floor for cash revenue collection as specified in the IMF agreement has not been met. In such circumstances it would be rational for policy makers to maximize revenues from privatisation.

Although it seems clear that political economy type of objectives are still of importance in most transition economies, the model outlined below can be used to analyse the relative shift in the objective function of policy makers towards the generation of revenues.

There are two strings of literature related to the topic of timing of privatisation. First, there is the literature on the issue of seasoned securities (equity) as pioneered by *Myers and Majluf (1984)* and developed further by *Krasker (1986)*. These papers use signalling models to describe equity issues. In particular, they show that whenever management has positive inside knowledge about the old assets of a firm, management might not want to issue new equity for a new investment project as then new shareholders might capture some of the returns of the old assets. However, there exist important differences to the model presented in this chapter. First of all, these papers assume that management maximizes the wealth of old shareholders, who keep their shares and who are assumed to be passive (i.e., they do not buy the new issue). In this model, only the proceeds from the sale are maximized. This also allows one to examine how the welfare of the old shareholders changes. Furthermore, it is assumed that the *percentage* of the equity sold by the state affects the value of the company (due to improved corporate governance) [1].

Secondly, *Leland and Pyle (1977)* analyse signalling by an entrepreneur who wants to go public, but does not sell 100% of the shares in order to signal the high quality of his firm. Here, the cost of signalling arises because the entrepreneur cannot diversify the project-specific risk optimally. However, the value of the project in their model does not depend on the amount of equity sold. In the model presented in this chapter there is a feed-back between the amount of equity sold and the value of the firms. Furthermore, if risk-averse agents were introduced, and assuming that the state is risk neutral, results exactly opposite to *Leland and Pyle* are obtained. For considerations of the firm inherent risk, it is more efficient for the state to hold on longer to the shares until that risk has decreased. More recently, *Rock (1986)* sparked a wave of papers on Initial Public Offerings. These models are mainly concerned to explain the apparent underpricing of new issues (relative to their subsequent valuation in the secondary market). Most of these models explain this phenomenon with rationing by an underwriter and often hinge on the modelling of the financial intermediary. However, the behaviour of underwriters does not seem to be crucial with respect to transition economies[2]. *Allan and Faulhaber (1989)* propose a model without underwriters where the firm has inside information. In their model firms can use underpricing as a signal that they are a good firm. Bad firms do not copy the behaviour of good firms, because only good firms can underprice and nevertheless pay a high dividend in the next period. Subsequently they sell further equity and get the price that is adequate for a good firm. Observing the low shareprices in transition economies it is tempting to examine whether low prices are used as signals. However, a price signal as in the *Allan and Faulhaber* model is not possible because the *state* obtains the proceeds, not the firms. Finally, *Perotti (1995)* applies a model to privatisation where the amount of shares a state owns in a firm serves as a commitment device not to interfere by adverse changes of regulatory policies. However, with respect to macroeconomic stabilisation, it is unlikely that such a commitment device is needed. Even after the state has sold all its firms there would still be very high costs of discontinuing macroeconomic stabilisations. Furthermore, in *Perotti*'s model governments cannot commit the following government to good policies. In unstable political situations as in transition economies, it is therefore more likely that governments signal information instead of restraining their actions. Further-

[1] It is also possible that the total revenue generated affects the value of the company due to a better chance of stabilizing the economy. However, this should be modelled in a political economy framework and not in a corporate finance setting.

[2] In transition economies there are often no underwriters involved in equity issues.

more, this model analyses the sale of a portfolio of firms. While complicating the signalling game this allows for some interesting results (which will in particular become clear when the existence of pooling equilibria is analysed)[3].

Against this background, my model focuses on questions different from those in the corporate finance literature. First, this chapter analyses whether the amount of privatisation can act as a screening device between good and bad firms still held by the state. This is linked to the question whether the state has an incentive to sell good or bad firms first. Second, it examines whether it can be optimal to sell all of the state-held shares immediately, or whether it can be rational to hold on to these shares for a longer time.

The chapter proceeds in the following way: In section 2.2, a model is presented where the state has inside information when selling its firms. In section 2.3 separating as well as pooling equilibria are constructed. Both equilibria are interpreted and their properties are examined. Section 2.4 examines the welfare effects of signalling. Section 2.5 reaches conclusions.

2.2 The Model

2.2.1 Agents

There are two agents, the state and investors. The state owns stakes in two firms, denoted by subscripts 0 and 1 respectively. Both holdings are normalized to 1. The state has already decided to sell its stakes to the investors, but it is not able to commit itself to do this under all circumstances. The state still has to decide about the time pattern of the sale.

2.2.2 Time Pattern

For simplicity it is assumed that there are only two time periods in which the state can sell shares of the firms. At t_0 the state determines a fraction of its holdings of firm 0 (a_0) and a fraction of its holdings of firm 1 (a_1) to be sold at t_0. Obviously, $0 \leq a_i \leq 1$. At t_1 the rest of the states' shareholdings $(1 - a_i)$ are sold off.

2.2.3 Firms

The two firms are of different types: one of the firms is good and one is bad (denoted by subscripts g and b, respectively). The variable s is a binary

[3] In the *Perotti* model, the state could signal its commitment by keeping some of the firms in its portfolio instead of using partial privatisation.

variable, which denotes which of the two firms is the good one. If s equals 0 firm 0 is good and if s equals 1 firm 1 is good. The value of a firm at the end of the game depends on its type. This type-dependent part is called f_i. Also, the value of both firms depends on the variable n, denoting the state of nature at t_1. Let V_{it} denote the value of firm i at time t. Its value at t_1 equals

$$V_{i1} = n + f_i(a_i), \forall i \in \{0,1\} \tag{2.1}$$

where

$$f_0'(a) \begin{matrix} > f_1'(a) \; for \; s = 0 \text{ (firm 0 is good)} \\ < f_1'(a) \; for \; s = 1 \text{ (firm 1 is good)} \end{matrix} \text{ and } f_0', f_1' > 0 \tag{2.2}$$

The first order derivatives of both type-specific parts of the firm values with respect to the amount of the shares sold, f_i', is positive, as gains from corporate governance make the firm the more valuable the more is sold to private investors at t_0. If $s = 0$, i.e. firm 0 is the good one, the marginal corporate governance gains from the sell-off are larger for firm 0 than for firm 1 and vice versa[4]. In particular, it is assumed that $f(a)$ has been linearised and therefore

$$f_i(a_i) = \beta_i + \gamma_i a_i, \forall i \in \{0,1\} \tag{2.3}$$

where β_i, γ_i are constants and $\gamma_g > \gamma_b > 0$. This means that the true value of a firm depends on the state of nature as captured by n, on a constant β according to its type, on the amount of shares sold off at t_0 as well as on a type-dependent constant γ. A motivation for this function can be found in appendix B[5]. In principal, it would not have to be the case that a linear function is chosen. While a closed solution without specifying $f(a)$ is not possible, the model could be solved for other specifications of $f(a)$. As long as this function has a positive first order derivative with respect to a, which is continuous, the results are robust. In particular, it is straightforward to see that a second order polynomial would lead to analogous results[6].

[4] In this sense, 'good' firm is a misnomer. To be more precise, a 'good' firm is a firm with large potential corporate governance gains.

[5] Essentially, it is a linearized version of a f(a) function derived in the framework of *Shleifer and Vishny (1986)*.

[6] However, in case the function f becomes discontinuous, the modelling becomes more complicated as different cases must be distinguished. In particular, if corporate governance gains only start after a minimum amount has been sold, this would imply that the state can only reach a separating equilibrium in case a sufficient amount of shares has been sold. The gains from such an equilibrium would then need to be traded off against selling more than would be consistent with the true value of n. Using such functions f would tend to put further restrictions on the existence of a separating equilibrium.

2.2.4 Information Structure

At t_0 nature draws the random variable n from the (ex-ante) cumulative distribution function $Q(n)$, defined from 0 to ∞. The ex-ante expected value of n is denoted by n^e. Nature also draws s which is 0 or 1 with equal probabilities. The two variables are independently distributed. Both variables are only observed by the state. At t_1, s and n are revealed to the market. The distribution of s, $Q(n)$, the objective function of the state and the functions f_i are common knowledge. The introduction of the variable s as a modelling device is helpful as it allows to specify both sources of uncertainty explicitly, which facilitates the notation of the model. It also clarifies that the problem the investors have to solve is one with two unknown variables and two signals, a_0 and a_1.

2.2.5 Strategies

The objective of the state is to maximize the present value of its revenues. Its strategy is a mapping of the two random variables s and n on a_0 and a_1:

$$S_S : \{s, n\} -> \{a_0, a_1\} \tag{2.4}$$

It is assumed that there is a large number of identical and risk-neutral investors who maximize their expected wealth at t_1. Furthermore, it is assumed that investors do not face any wealth constraints. The two assets are the only ones available to investors apart from the risk-free asset which yields the known interest rate r. Therefore, they demand all the shares the state issues if the expected yield is greater than, or equal to, r. They demand nothing if the expected yield is smaller than r [7]. If two investors offer the same amount for an asset, a coin is tossed to determine the new owner[8]. The strategy of the investors is the following: at t_0 they will bid h_{i0} for each firm and at t_1 they will bid h_{i1} for firm 0 and 1. Their strategy is a mapping of a_0 and a_1 on the prices they pay in the two periods:

$$S_{inv} : \{a_0, a_1\} -> \{h_{00}, h_{01}, h_{10}, h_{11}\} \tag{2.5}$$

[7] Instead of a perfectly competitive environment it can be assumed that two homogeneous investors act in a Bertrand fashion. This would result in the same outcome but is presumably a more realistic description of the market for privatized firms.

[8] Given these assumptions all investors will always bid the same amount and the winner will always be determined by the toss of a coin. However, this chapter does not focus on which investor will buy the shares. For an examination of these issues see *Cornelli and Lee, 1995.*

Given that at t_1 all information is public and investors behave competitively, h_{i1} will exactly equal $(1 - a_i)V_{i1}$, i.e. the true value of the remaining shares up for sale. Therefore, the focus is on the strategies of investors at t_0,

$$S_{inv'} = \{a_0, a_1\} -> \{h_{00}, h_{10}\} \tag{2.6}$$

Having observed how much the state sells in each firm, investors update their beliefs conditioning on these signals. Their conditional beliefs are a mapping that associates each pair of quantities a_0, a_1 with probability functions $p(.|a_0, a_1)$ on [0,1] where $p(s|a_0, a_1)$ is the probability investors attach to the type of firm, i.e. to the value of s, given the two quantities sold at t_0. Similarly, $Q(.|a_0, a_1)$ denotes the cumulative probability function of n, the state of nature dependent part of the firms' values, after investors have observed a_0 and a_1.

In the context of the second stage of the Russian privatisation program, this model can be interpreted in the following way: n can be thought of as representing the state of nature at t_1, a large n resembling a good (reformist) state and a low n a bad (reactionist) state. At t_0, policy makers know better than anyone else how influential they will be in the next period. Therefore, they can make a more informed judgement on whether t_1 will be a reformist state of nature or not. Alternatively, the value of n could depend on some unobservable characteristics of policy makers: only they themselves know their personal objective function. The assumption that the state has superior information on the type of firm can be justified because the state has been the owner of the assets for the last decades and often still owns a considerable amount of the shares. Furthermore, the state is likely to have some inside information on how good the management of a particular firm is, given that management had been installed by the state. In this case the state has inside knowledge about potential gains from corporate governance, at least vis-a-vis outside investors. Privatisation is assumed to improve the corporate governance mechanism so as to increase profits of the privatized firms. This is in line with empirical findings of *Boardman and Vining (1989)*. Therefore it is the sell-off as such which affects the valuation of the firm. Furthermore, the larger the stake an outside investor buys in the firm, the more likely it is that he is powerful enough to improve the firm's performance[9]. However, in Russia, most of the firms in which shares were sold during the second stage of privatisation, had already private owners as shares had been sold to insiders and in voucher auctions to the population. Would an additional sell-off nevertheless improve efficiency ? As the first stage of privatisation has failed to create major blockholders, it can be argued that it was only the second stage, that would create blockholders, which in turn would tend to monitor management more closely and make the firms more efficient. This

[9] See also appendix B for a theoretical derivation as well as Chapter 3 for some related empirical findings.

would in particular be the case given the evidence provided in the introduction on how management was aiming to prevent the sales of workers' shares to outsiders, i.e. the creation of blockholders on the secondary market. Interestingly, *Boardman and Vining* provide some evidence that enterprises in mixed ownership also perform worse than 100% private firms. While their evidence is not clear on whether mixed ownership firms perform better or worse than state owned firms, this finding would indicate that there should be substantial efficiency gains from further sell offs.

Given this interpretation of n and $f(a)$, the question could be raised whether f should not depend on n. And indeed it seems plausible that the extent of the benefits of corporate governance depend on the state of nature at t_1. However, to simplify the analysis, the problem can be thought of as having been linearised in a way as to separate the two different sources of uncertainty over the final value of the firms. This does not seem to be too strong an assumption as conceptually, the solution of the model does not change. As long as investors know the functions $f_g(a,n)$ and $f_b(a,n)$ and the corporate governance gains of the same firm are larger in all states of nature n, they fundamentally still have a problem of 2 unknowns and 2 signals to solve[10].

2.2.6 Equilibrium Concept

Given the structure of the model, an equilibrium can be calculated based on the strategies defined above. A Perfect Bayesian Equilibrium in this context is a pair of strategies $(S_S, S_{inv'})$ and conditional beliefs $p(.|a_0,a_1)$ and $Q(.|a_0,a_1)$, such that

(i) for all $\{a_0,a_1\}$ in the range of S_S , $p(.|a_0,a_1)$ is the conditional probability of s, and $Q(.|a_0,a_1)$ is the conditional cumulative probability function for n, obtained by updating the prior probability distributions $(\frac{1}{2}, \frac{1}{2})$ and $Q(n)$ respectively, using $\{a_0,a_1\}$ in a Bayesian fashion.

(ii) for all $\{a_0,a_1\}$ and assuming that there exists a function mapping a_0 and a_1 to h_{00} and h_{01}

$$h_{i0}(a_0,a_1) = \frac{\int_0^\infty ndQ(.|a_0,a_1) + f_g(a_i)p(s=i|a_0,a_1) + f_b(a_i)p(s \neq i|a_0,a_1)}{1+r}, \tag{2.7}$$

$\forall i \in \{0.1\}$.

(iii) for all $\{s,n\}$

[10] For example, in case f_i is of the following form: $f_i(a,n) = d_i + g_i a_i + h_i n_i + i_i a_i n_i$ $\forall i \in \{g,b\}$ with h_i, i_i being some constants, such that $\frac{\partial f_g}{\partial a} > \frac{\partial f_b}{\partial a}$ *for all* n, the solution to the model would be exactly analogous to the case analyzed.

$$a_i \in \arg\max_{a_i} \sum_{i=0}^{1} [a_i h_{i0}(a_0, a_1) + \frac{1-a_i}{1+r} V_{i1}(a_i)], \forall i \in \{0,1\} \tag{2.8}$$

Condition (i) stipulates that investors have rational expectations, conditions (ii) and (iii) are the requirements that investors as well as the state are optimising (given rational beliefs). The argument concerning the optimization of investors is the following[11]: given that at least two homogeneous investors compete in a Bertrand fashion, they know that they will only obtain the shares, if they bid more or equal to the discounted expected value of V_{i1}, using a_0 and a_1 to make inferences. However, they never bid any more than this expected value since they would expect to incur a loss. Their expected value of the firm is the expected value of n using their conditional belief $Q(.|a_0, a_1)$ plus the expected value of f using the conditional beliefs $p(.|a_0, a_1)$. Condition (iii) states that the state chooses the amount it sells in each firm in a way which maximizes total revenues from the sales at t_0 and t_1, given the prices the investors are going to bid after they observed the amounts sold. Based on this equilibrium concept the following section will derive the three different equilibria that fulfil these criteria.

2.3 Separating and Pooling Equilibria

In this section three different kinds of equilibria will be proposed and motivated. The analysis is similar to traditional rational expectations models (e.g. *Kyle, 1985*). The key difference from a technical point of view is that two different signals are sent as opposed to one. The two signals can be consistent or inconsistent with each other.

PROPOSITION 2.1: For a finite n, there exists a unique separating Perfect Bayesian Equilibrium. S_s and $S_{inv'}$ are given by:

$$\{a_s = e^{-\frac{n}{\gamma_g}}, a_{i \neq s} = e^{-\frac{n}{\gamma_b}}\}, \tag{2.9}$$

$$\{h_{00} = \frac{-\gamma_g \ln(a_0) + f_g(a_0)}{1+r}, h_{10} = \frac{-\gamma_b \ln(a_1) + f_b(a_1)}{1+r}\} \text{ if } a_0 > a_1 \tag{2.10}$$

$$\{h_{00} = \frac{-\gamma_b \ln(a_0) + f_b(a_0)}{1+r}, h_{10} = \frac{-\gamma_g \ln(a_1) + f_g(a_1)}{1+r}\} \text{ if } a_0 < a_1$$

under the following two conditions[12]:

[11] This is a simplification as it allows not to model the utility function of the investors explicitly.

[12] It needs to be noted that conditions 2.11 and 2.12 could equivalently be written in a form which uses a_0 and a_1 instead of n.

$$(\beta_g - \beta_b) < (\gamma_g - \gamma_b)(1 - \sum_{i \in \{g,b\}} e^{-\frac{n}{\gamma_i}}) \tag{2.11}$$

$$n > m_{\max}, \tag{2.12}$$

where $m_{\max}$, formally defined in appendix A, denotes the value of n that makes the state exactly indifferent between signalling the true n by holding on to a part of the shares on the one hand and selling off all shares in both firms at t_0 on the other hand. The proof for this proposition is provided in appendix A.

In this equilibrium, different amounts of shares of the two companies are sold. The state keeps holding a fraction of its shares in each firm. This allows investors to identify the type of each firm. Given that investors know a firm's type they can use either signal (a_0 or a_1) to learn the value of n. The two signals are consistent with each other in equilibrium. Consequently, the investors' bids are equal to the true value of each firm. The equilibrium is fully revealing. The two conditions 2.11 and 2.12 will be examined in more detail following proposition 2.5. They are derived in appendix A. Intuitively, (2.11) can be interpreted as a condition under which the state has no incentive to cheat by sending a wrong signal about which firm is of which type. If this condition does not hold the state can not credibly commit itself to do so because the gains from fooling investors are larger than losses from inefficient corporate governance for the good firm. Condition 2.12 states that the separating equilibrium breaks down if the true value of n is so small that the gains from signalling to investors are outweighed by the corporate governance gains from selling off all shares at t_0.

Furthermore, there exist two different pooling equilibria:

PROPOSITION 2.2: There exists a unique pooling Perfect Bayesian Equilibrium where the state holds on to some of its shares ($a_0 = a_1 \equiv a < 1$). S_s and $S_{inv'}$ are given by:

$$a = e^{-\frac{2n}{\gamma_g + \gamma_b}} \tag{2.13}$$

$$\{h_{00} = \frac{-(\gamma_g + \gamma_b)\ln(a) + \sum_{i \in \{g,b\}} f_i(a)}{2(1+r)}, h_{10} = h_{00}\} \tag{2.14}$$

This PBE exists if condition 2.11 does not hold and condition 2.12 does. The proof for this proposition is provided in appendix A.

In this equilibrium, the same amount of shares is sold in both firms. Consequently, investors cannot infer which firm is of which type. They therefore use their priors (equal probability of each firm being the good one) to determine their bids. The state again sells less than 100% of its shares signalling the true n to investors. While the state would prefer a separating equilibrium, it cannot credibly commit to sell more of the good firm if condition 2.11 does not hold. If condition 2.12 holds, the state prefers not to sell off everything at t_0. This is not true in the third equilibrium:

PROPOSITION 2.3: There exists a pooling Perfect Bayesian Equilibrium where all shares are sold off immediately. Then S_s is {1,1} and $S_{inv'}$ is:

$$\{h_{00} = \frac{2n_m + \sum_{i\in\{g,b\}} f_i(a)}{2(1+r)}, h_{10} = h_{00}\} \tag{2.15}$$

It exists whenever condition 2.12 does not hold.

Proof: If the state decided not to signal anything about n (by, for example deducting an arbitrarily small ε from either a_0 or a_1, such that n cannot be inferred in a consistent manner) investors' beliefs about n are n_m as defined in appendix A. Given these beliefs it is optimal for the state not to signal n but to collect the complete corporate governance gains by selling off all shares (apart from ε) at t_0 iff $R_N > R_S$ in the case of a separating equilibrium and if $R_N > R_P$ in the case of a pooling equilibrium. This is exactly true, if condition 2.12 does not hold, as can be seen in appendix A. The updating of investors' beliefs about n from n^e to n_m is rational since n_m is exactly the expected value for n given that it is rational for the state not to signal anything.□

In this equilibrium all shares are sold at t_0 and investors cannot distinguish between the two firms. As pointed out above, this is to be the case whenever the gains from signalling n are outweighed by the corporate governance gains from selling off all shares at t_0.

PROPOSITION 2.4

(a) In the separating as well as in the pooling equilibria, more shares are sold in each firm the worse the state of nature, i.e. a_0 and a_1 are the larger the smaller n.

(b) In the separating as well as in the pooling equilibrium described in proposition 2.2 the amount of shares the state optimally sells is larger the larger the marginal gains from corporate governance, γ_g and γ_b. It is ambiguous, though, if larger γ_g and γ_b increase the likelihood of reaching equilibria where *all* shares are sold, as described in proposition 2.3.

Proof: (a) can easily be verified by calculating the partial derivatives of equations 3.17 and 2.13. Furthermore, if condition 2.12 does not hold, the state sets $a_0 = a_1 = 1$. Condition 2.12 is less likely to hold if n is small. However, it is not clear whether condition 2.12 is also less likely to hold for large γ_i. Totally differentiating condition 2.32 shows that this depends on the ex-ante distribution of n.

$$\frac{dm}{dg_i} = -\frac{2\frac{\partial E(n|n\leq m)}{\partial m} - 2 + e^{-\frac{m}{\gamma_g}} + e^{-\frac{m}{\gamma_b}}}{1-(1+\frac{m}{\gamma_i})e^{-\frac{m}{\gamma_i}}}, \forall i \in \{g,b\} \tag{2.16}$$

While the denominator is unambiguously positive, the sign of the nominator depends on N. □

An intuitive explanation is that there is a trade-off between selling at t_0 and obtaining the benefits from better corporate governance on the one hand and keeping some of the shares such that the market believes that the state really has inside information that justifies higher prices on the other. If the state sold off everything at t_0, the market would think that n is small which will depress shareprices. Also, because the benefits from better corporate governance differ between good and bad firms, it can be optimal for the state to choose a_g different from a_b. In that case a fully revealing separating equilibrium is obtained in which the state sells more of the good firm. The market (knowing f_i) is then able to distinguish between good and bad firms. This is a natural equilibrium, as the corporate governance gains that are not made if the state holds on to its shares are larger for the good firm. The reason why the equilibrium is fully revealing is simple. There are two signals (a_0 and a_1) and two unknowns: n and s. With two equations and two unknowns the investors can in general infer the two unknowns from the action of the state. Only when the state destroys the signalling equilibrium (if $n < m_{\max}$) is the equilibrium not fully revealing.

It could be argued that the above equilibria are not credible as the state has an incentive to sell a positive amount of shares directly after it sold the first batch at t_0. However, in reality this is unlikely. It seems reasonable to expect an exogenously given minimum period of time dt between two sales. This positive dt could be caused, for example, by the process of organizing an auction or by legislation that needs to be passed before each sale[13]. This dt, in particular in transition economies, could be substantial. Given that $dt > 0$, it is possible to find equilibria similar to the ones described in propositions 2.1 to 2.3. This is true as the state still incurs a cost of signalling, equivalent to the present value of obtaining the corporate governance benefits only at t_0+dt instead of at t_0. A further cost to the state would be the fact that in a follow-up auction, the winner of the first auction would have some bargaining power. This is true because the way the corporate governance gains are motivated (see appendix B) relies on the fact that one investor obtains the whole package of shares that is sold by the state. Without having homogeneous investors competing for the shares, the state would not be able to extract all the gains from improved corporate governance.

The three equilibria are mutually exclusive. Their existence depend on the two conditions 2.11 and 2.12. The next proposition describes how different parameters affect the likelihood of different equilibria, followed by a more detailed interpretation of the two conditions.

PROPOSITION 2.5: A separating equilibria is more likely

(a) the smaller the type-specific value independent of corporate governance of the good firm and the larger the one of the bad firm, i.e. the smaller β_g and the larger β_b, and

(b) the better the state of nature, i.e. the larger n, as long as $n>m_{\max}$.

[13] Alternatively a fixed cost of having an auction could be assumed, which should give a similar result.

(c) A separating equilibrium can be more or less likely with respect to the marginal gains from corporate governance, γ_g and γ_b, depending on $Q(n)$ and n.

Proof: Part (a) is true as the partial derivative of the left hand side of condition 2.11 with respect to β_g is positive and negative with respect to β_b. Part (b) is trivially true due to condition 2.12, as $m_{\max}$ does not depend on n. Furthermore, the signs of the derivatives of the right-hand-side of condition 2.11 with respect to γ_i depend on n and, as shown in appendix A on $Q(n)$. □

Condition 2.11 is a condition under which the state tells the truth: if it does not hold the state cannot commit credibly to sell more of the good firm than of the bad firm. Then investors anticipate that the state has an incentive to cheat. Therefore the investors would value the firm of which a large stake is sold as if it was the bad firm. A pooling equilibrium results. This is more likely if $(\beta_g - \beta_b)$ is positive and relatively large and if γ_g is relatively small and γ_b relatively large. This is true, because by cheating the state realises less of the corporate governance gains but obtains more of β_g and less of β_b by fooling the market. Furthermore, the incentive to cheat is larger if a relatively large stake is sold of the bad firm and a relatively small stake of the good firm. In that case the punishment for cheating is smaller as the state realizes less corporate governance gains at t_1. This happens if γ_g is relatively large and γ_b is relatively small. Therefore the signs of the respective derivatives with respect to γ_g and γ_b are unclear.

If condition 2.12 does not hold, the corporate governance gains from selling the states' stakes off at t_0 outweigh the potential gains from signalling the correct n. Therefore, it is optimal for the state to sell off everything and no separating equilibrium exists. As is expected, the larger n, the more likely is condition 2.12 to hold. Furthermore, it should be noted that if condition 2.12 holds, the state obtains the full value of the firm, including the gains that will accrue due to better corporate governance. This is a result of the assumption of perfect competition among symmetric investors.

The state never prefers a pooling equilibrium to a separating one (if $\gamma_g \neq \gamma_b$) if the separating one can be obtained. This is true as a pooling equilibrium places one more restriction on the maximization problem of the state. However, this is not sufficient to demonstrate that the state cannot do worse in a separating equilibrium because the beliefs of the investors are defined in a different way for the case of a pooling equilibrium. However, appendix A demonstrates that it is nevertheless true. This is an interesting result because it also indicates that it can be rational from the point of view of a revenue maximizing state to split up its firms into different units before selling them off. A pooling equilibrium exists when either condition 2.11 or 2.12 does not hold. In particular, when condition 2.12 does not hold, a corner solution results where everything is sold at t_0. As long as n is a finite number and $\gamma_i > 0, \forall i \in \{0,1\}$, a corner solution where $a_0 = a_1 = 0$ will not exist. The state therefore always has an incentive to sell some of its shares.

To sum up, the model shows that it might be *rational* to sell different stakes in different firms in order to maximize revenues in a situation of asymmetric information. Shares of firms with smaller gains due to corporate governance are held by the state until the informational asymmetries are reduced. A pooling equilibrium only exists if the state has important inside information varying significantly across individual firms' assets, irrespective of potential corporate governance gains, or when the state does not expect the future to be very bright.

2.4 Social Welfare

Clearly, the above outcome is second best. The costs of signalling are the following:

PROPOSITION 2.6:

(a) There are positive costs of signalling whenever the state of nature in period 2 is 'too' good, i.e. if $n > m_{\max}$.

(b) The costs in the pooling equilibrium of proposition 2.2 exceed the ones in the separating equilibrium.

Proof: A simple maximization of V_{01} and V_{11} with respect to a_0 and a_1 demonstrates that the value maximizing strategy of the state is: $S_{S\max} = \{1,1\}$. The strategies of investors do not affect the value of the firms. $S_{S\max}$ only leads to a Nash-equilibrium when condition 2.12 does not hold.

Under $S_{S\max}$ the values of the two firms at t_1 equal

$$\sum_{i\in\{0,1\}} V_{i1} = \sum_{i\in\{g,b\}} [n + f_i(1)] = \sum_{i\in\{g,b\}} [n + \beta_i + \gamma_i] \tag{2.17}$$

If condition 2.12 does not hold, this value is smaller by C, a pure welfare loss.

$$\begin{aligned} C(n,\gamma_g,\gamma_b) &= \sum_{i\in\{0,1\}} \gamma_i(1 - e^{-\frac{n}{\gamma_g}}) && \text{if (2.11) holds} \\ C(n,\gamma_g,\gamma_b) &= \sum_{i\in\{0,1\},j\neq i} \gamma_i(1 - e^{-\frac{2n}{\gamma_g+\gamma_b}}) && \text{if (2.11) does not hold} \end{aligned} \tag{2.18}$$

Using the result in appendix A, the former is smaller than the latter. □

COROLLARY 2.1: For each type of equilibrium, the costs of signalling are larger the better the state of nature at t_1 and the larger the marginal gains of corporate governance γ_0 and γ_1.

Proof: The partial derivatives of $C(\cdot)$ with respect to n are positive in the separating equilibrium of proposition 2.1 as well as in the pooling equilibrium of proposition 2.2. However, it is not possible to make a global statement on n, i.e. on costs across different equilibria. While from proposition 2.6 a positive welfare cost is more likely the larger n, the welfare costs could also be affected by a switch from the separating equilibrium of proposition 2.1 to the pooling equilibrium of proposition 2.3 due to a change in n. From proposition 2.5 a separating equilibrium is more likely than a pooling equilibrium the larger n and from proposition 2.6 the welfare costs of a separating equilibrium are smaller than the costs of a pooling one. This allows only for statements for a specific equilibrium.

The partial derivatives with respect to γ_i are

$$\begin{array}{ll} \frac{\partial C}{\partial g_i} = 1 - e^{-\frac{n}{\gamma_i}}(1 + \frac{n}{\gamma_i}), \forall i \in \{g, b\} & if\ (2.11) \text{ holds and} \\ \frac{\partial C}{\partial g_i} = 1 - e^{-\frac{2n}{\gamma_g + \gamma_b}}(1 + \frac{2 g_i n}{\gamma_g + \gamma_b}), \forall i \in \{g, b\} & if\ (2.11) \text{ does not hold} \end{array} \quad (2.19)$$

Both partial derivatives are positive. This implies that the costs of signalling strictly increase with γ_i whenever $n > m_{\max}$. However, from proposition 2.4 it is not clear whether larger γ_i leads to the equilibrium of proposition 2.3 more often. Therefore, it is not possible to make a global statement about γ_i. □.

The intuition is the following: The larger n the fewer shares of the firms are sold at t_0 which increases the welfare cost. With respect to γ_i there are two effects, which are partly offsetting: On the one hand, the amount that is sold is larger the larger γ. On the other hand, the welfare cost from each unit not privatized increases the larger γ. The direct welfare reducing effect of a larger γ dominates the indirect effect.

Having shown the existence of a dead-weight loss, the question arises whether there could be a non-dissipative equilibrium. If it was possible to signal n in another (and cheaper) way than by holding on to share-packages, the dead-weight loss could be reduced. However, it is very unclear, what could be a different and cheaper signalling device. *Grundy and Constantinides (1989)* construct a non-dissipative signalling equilibrium, where a firm issues a security to finance investment as well as a stock repurchase. However, in our case an efficient equilibrium requires that the state gets rid of all voting rights of its stake and (to avoid principal-agent problems) also of all income rights attached to its shares. Therefore, it is not straight-forward to construct a non-dissipative signalling equilibrium along these lines.

Interpreting the model above very strictly (that is n will be in fact revealed to everyone at t_1 and a similar problem does not arise between t_1 and t_2), there exists a very simple solution. An investor obtains all the shares in both firms for the price of $f_i(1)$ and a contract is written where the investor promises to pay $2n$ at t_1, i.e. after the true n has been revealed. In practice, firms could be asked to make a payment at t_1 amounting to the change in the value between t_0 and t_1 of a stock-market index consisting of firms that had already been completely private before. However, there is a problem with this solution. If this contract was written, it would probably lead to asset stripping from the investor between t_0 and t_1 as the investor can not commit himself to pay up at t_1. Subsequently, the investor would either disappear or go bankrupt. Secondly, if investors were wealth constrained, they would be unlikely to buy both firms. If they were also risk-averse, the proceeds for the state would be smaller, as there would be no way to signal which firm is good and which one is bad. On the other hand, the government could tell the markets n and commit itself to pay back the difference between the true n and the announced one at time t_1 (adjusted for interest). But again, the government is unlikely to be able to commit itself, in particular as there might be a different government in power at t_1 (generating the fluctuations in n in the first place). Therefore, it appears likely that a second best result will be obtained due to asymmetric information and the non-contractibility of n.

Lastly, the effect of the sale on the welfare of the old shareholders needs to be analysed by examining changes in shareprices at the date of the announcement of the extent of the sales. The share-price directly prior to the announcement for each of the two firms is

$$V_{old}^{S} = \frac{2n^e + \sum_{i \in \{0,1\}} \beta_i + \gamma_i e^{-\frac{n^e}{\gamma_i}}}{2(1+r)} \tag{2.20}$$

if conditions 2.11 and 2.12 hold with n replaced by n^e. If condition 2.11 does not hold but condition 2.12 does with n replaced by n^e then the share-price would be

$$V_{old}^{P} = \frac{2n^e + \sum_{i \in \{0,1\}, j \neq i} \beta_i + \gamma_i e^{-\frac{2n^e}{\gamma_i + \gamma_j}}}{2(1+r)} \tag{2.21}$$

If condition 2.12 does not hold (replacing n by n^e), the shareprice would have been

$$V_{old}^{P'} = \frac{2n_m + \sum_{i \in \{g,b\}} \beta_i + \gamma_i}{2(1+r)} \tag{2.22}$$

The changes in the shareprices at the announcement of S_S at t_0 depend on the following: if conditions 2.11 and 2.12 hold for the true n, there are two effects. First, prices rise for one firm and fall for the other one as it is revealed which one is good. However, this effect could be more than offset by new information on n. If investors infer that $n > n^e$ prices could move upwards for all firms and downwards if $n < n^e$. However, they will not move upwards by the whole extent of the higher revealed n because a higher than expected n means that fewer corporate governance gains than expected are to be realized. If condition 2.11 or 2.12 does not hold for the true n, there is only the second effect.

2.5 Conclusion

This chapter offers an explanation for why a rational government committed to full scale privatisation might nevertheless retain some of its shares. It is argued in the context of a signalling model that this could happen because the state needs to signal to the assets' buyers its inside information about the future value of those assets. The trade-off is then between selling shares immediately and obtaining the benefits from better corporate governance on the one hand and keeping some of the shares such that the market believes that the state really has inside information that justifies higher prices on the other. Furthermore, it is argued that the larger the gains from corporate governance (resulting from the sell-off) at that particular firm, the more of its shares are sold. Differing benefits from better corporate governance lead to differing costs of keeping the shares in state ownership and it would therefore be rational for the state to sell off different amounts in each firm. The model provides a competing theory to the explanations offered for partial privatisation (mostly in the context of Western economies). However, this model would be consistent with the argument of insufficient liquidity as a reason for partial privatisation if low liquidity was due to substantial asymmetric information. The model also provides a competing theory to the political economy explanations put forward for transition economies.

The model relies crucially on the assumption that the state is maximizing revenues from privatisation. While the introduction to this chapter has made the case for this assumption, it is nevertheless interesting to analyse different cases. Clearly, the set-up of this model does not allow for any other objectives of the state. In particular, if the state was indifferent with respect to privatisation revenues, there would be no need to signal the true value of the firms. If the state instead cared about social welfare, it would sell off all shares immediately to maximize the gains from improved corporate governance. In case the privatisation program was driven exclusively by political considerations, the state would presumably allocate the shares to the group that is politically required to be bought off. However, it is important to realize that it is possible that political considerations (or social welfare considerations) are merely added constraints on the privatisation program, which still aims to maximize revenues. In that case the state would still solve the maximization problem described in section 2.2.6 under some additional constraints. *Boycko et al* imply that this was the underlying rationale for the Russian privatisation program in aggregate. While political constraints were fulfilled in the first stage of privatisation with its focus on insiders and the population, the second stage of privatisation might better reflect the intentions of the creators of the privatisation program. However, even during the second stage there might still be some political constraints existing.

The above model offers different starting points for empirical investigations. First, the model implies that governments should sell more shares in firms where the potential gains from corporate governance are large. It seems impractical to test this hypothesis as higher corporate governance gains (which could be measured by the shareprice performance) also can *result* from a larger extent of privatisation. Therefore, a system of equations would have to be specified and it is not clear whether the system could be identified. More interestingly, governments should hold on to their shares if they believe that the future macroeconomic state will be a good one. This would generate a pattern at odds with received wisdom. If an index of firms whose ownership structure remained unchanged over the sampling period was constructed, it could be tested whether these firms would perform better in countries where the state retained more of the shares in the privatized companies. Of course, many other factors would presumably need to be controlled for.

Alternatively, it would be possible to carry out event studies on the day of the announcements of the sale (and on the days of the sale). In the context of a pooling equilibrium (the same amount of shares are sold in different firms) prices should tend to fall in cases in which more shares are sold than expected and tend to rise if fewer shares than expected are sold. This is, of course, exactly what is in general observed. However, usually it is attributed to low liquidity of the markets and not directly to informational issues. However, 'low liquidity' might be just another label for the same story. After all, there is an extensive literature on how asymmetric information causes the market to be illiquid (e.g. *Glosten and Milgrom, 1985*). If insiders are known to be in the market, market makers have to protect themselves against the possibility of trading with insiders (and losing money on these trades). They therefore demand a high spread between their bid and ask price and also adjust their prices downward if large blocks are to be sold. This means that it is expensive to sell a security, in particular in large quantities. This, in turn, is the essence of what is called an illiquid market. In the case of Russia, demand for these securities could potentially be very high (as capital flight worth several billion USD per year is occurring and foreigners are principally free to invest) and prices in 1996 were very low *(Nash and Willer, 1995)*. In this context asymmetric information is likely to be an important reason for downward pressure on prices when large blocks of shares are to be sold. It also could explain why prices remain low after the sell-off.

2.6 Appendix A

2.6.1 Proof of Proposition 2.1

Suppose without loss of generality that $a_0 > a_1$. The two first-order conditions of the state's optimization problem following from equation 2.8 are:

$$h_{i0} + a_i \frac{\partial h_{i0}}{\partial a_i} + \frac{1 - a_i}{1 + r} \frac{\partial V_{i1}}{\partial a_i} - \frac{1}{1 + r} V_{i1} + a_j \frac{\partial h_{j0}}{\partial a_i} = 0, \forall i \in \{0, 1\}, j \neq i \quad (2.23)$$

Both $\frac{\partial h_{00}}{\partial a_1}$ and $\frac{\partial h_{10}}{\partial a_0}$ are discontinuous functions. A change in the amount of firm 1's shares sold can affect the valuation of firm 0 and vice versa. This can be achieved either by destroying the mechanism used to update the beliefs about n due to inconsistency or by changing the beliefs about the type of firm. It will be shown below that under conditions 2.11 and 2.12 it is not optimal to affect the valuation in this way. Therefore, these partial derivatives can be disregarded for now. In a fully revealing equilibrium it must be true that

$$h_{i0} = \frac{1}{1+r} V_{i1}, \forall i \in \{0,1\} \tag{2.24}$$

Now it is assumed that investors believe that the firm of which more shares are sold is the good firm. Later it will be shown that there can be no equilibrium where more shares of the bad firm are sold. Equations 2.23, 2.24 and 3.15 then result in

$$\frac{\partial h_{00}}{\partial a_0} = \frac{1}{1+r}(1 - \frac{1}{a_0})\gamma_g \text{ and } \frac{\partial h_{10}}{\partial a_1} = \frac{1}{1+r}(1 - \frac{1}{a_1})\gamma_b \tag{2.25}$$

Integrating equation 2.25 results in

$$h_{00} = \frac{-\gamma_g \ln(a_0) + \gamma_g a_0}{1+r} + C_0 \text{ and } h_{10} = \frac{-\gamma_b \ln(a_1) + \gamma_b a_1}{1+r} + C_1 \tag{2.26}$$

where C_0 and C_1 are integration constants. The constants C_0 and C_1 can be determined by further equilibrium considerations. Suppose that in a signalling equilibrium the state set a_0=1-ε, where ε is an arbitrarily small amount, and a_1=1-δ, where $\delta > \varepsilon$, then, in the limit as ε goes to 0, it must be true that

$$h_{00} = \frac{\beta_g + \gamma_g}{1+r} \tag{2.27}$$

If it was smaller than this value, competition among investors would drive the price up. If it was any larger, the state could sell firms for a price higher than their present value whenever the true n was close enough to 0. This can not be the case in a fully revealing equilibrium[14]. Therefore

$$C_0 = \frac{\beta_g}{1+r} \tag{2.28}$$

The same line of argument holds for δ approaching 0, which results in

$$C_1 = \frac{\beta_b}{1+r} \tag{2.29}$$

Substituting the value of these constants into equation 2.26 results in equation 2.10. Substituting equation 2.10 into equation 2.23 and again disregarding the cross derivatives results in the optimal strategies for the state

[14] It should be noted that the beliefs that determine the integration constants are out of equilibrium beliefs whenever m_{max} >0.

as stated in equation 3.17. Therefore, the belief of the investors that more of the good firm is sold off has been confirmed. It is easily shown that beliefs of investors that more of the bad firm is sold would not be confirmed and therefore cannot form an equilibrium.

It still needs to be verified under which conditions $\frac{\partial h_{10}}{\partial a_0}$ and $\frac{\partial h_{00}}{\partial a_1}$ can be disregarded. The state can affect the valuation of firm j by its choice of a_i in three different ways. First, it can change the investor's perception of which firm is good and which one is bad. Therefore, for the equilibrium above to hold it needs to be verified that the state has no incentive to sell more of the bad firm than of the good firm (that is to cheat). Telling the truth, the state receives the revenues R_S:

$$R_S = \frac{2n + \sum_{i \in \{g,b\}} [\beta_i + \gamma_i e^{-\frac{n}{\gamma_i}}]}{1+r} \tag{2.30}$$

Cheating would imply that the state sells $e^{-\frac{n}{\gamma_g}}$ of the bad firm and $e^{-\frac{n}{\gamma_b}}$ of the good firm at t_0. The investors then mistake the good firm for the bad firm. Only at t_1 investors learn which firm is good and which is bad. This would result in state revenues of R_C:

$$R_C = \frac{\sum_{i \in \{g,b\}, j \neq i} [e^{-\frac{n}{\gamma_i}}(n + \beta_i + \gamma_i e^{-\frac{n}{\gamma_i}}) + (1 - e^{-\frac{n}{\gamma_i}})(n + \beta_j + \gamma_j e^{-\frac{n}{\gamma_j}})]}{1+r} \tag{2.31}$$

It can be easily shown that $R_C < R_S$ iff condition 2.11 holds. Second, the state can affect the valuation of firm j by its choice of a_i if it chose a_i such that the two possible Bayesian updating procedures with the help of the two different a's would imply different n's. In this case of inconsistency, the signalling property of the equilibrium breaks down. What are investors to believe in this case ? The rational beliefs for investors in this case are derived by calculating a cut-off value for n (called $m_{\max}$) that makes the state just indifferent between signalling and selling off all shares without signalling. This is slightly complicated by the fact that there exists also a pooling equilibrium, as described by proposition 2.2, where the state sells off the same amount of shares in each firm and also signals the true n. Therefore, two cases must be distinguished. In the first line of equation 2.32, which is applicable if condition 2.12 holds for the value of n in question, the right-hand-side represents the revenues in the separating equilibrium of proposition 2.1. The right-hand-side in the second line, under the condition that a separating equilibrium does not exist for the n under question, represents the revenues in the case of a pooling equilibrium (as shown in proposition 2.2). The left hand side of equation 2.32 is the amount of revenue if the state sells off all shares without signalling, given the rational beliefs for n in the absence of signalling. If both revenues are equal, the state is indifferent between selling off everything at t_0 and signalling the true n. The largest n for which this would be true is then used by the investors to make inferences about the true n in the absence of signalling. It is called n_m and equals the conditional expectation of n given that the true n must be smaller than the largest n that would make the state indifferent between signalling and not signalling.

More formally, let M denote a set containing 0 and all positive values for m that satisfy

$$\begin{aligned} &2E(n|n \leq m) + \sum_{i\in\{g,b\}} \gamma_i = 2m + \sum_{i\in\{0,1\}} \gamma_i e^{-\frac{m}{\gamma_i}} \\ &if\ (\beta_g - \beta_b) < (\gamma_g - \gamma_b)(1 - \sum_{i\in\{g,b\}} \gamma_i e^{-\frac{m}{\gamma_i}}) \\ &2E(n|n \leq m) + \sum_{i\in\{g,b\}} \gamma_i = 2m + \sum_{i\in\{0,1\}} \gamma_i e^{-\frac{2m}{\gamma_g+\gamma_b}} \\ &otherwise \end{aligned} \tag{2.32}$$

Let $m_{\max}$ be the largest element in M. Furthermore, define n_m as $E(n|n \leq m_{\max})$. If n is larger than $m_{\max}$ it does not make sense for the state to signal given that n_m are the beliefs about n in the absence of signalling. Whether there are any elements in M apart from 0 depends on the ex-ante distribution of n, $Q(n)$.

The state would have an incentive to forego the possibility of signalling n when the corporate governance gains from selling everything at t_0 would more than outweigh the higher n signalled by retaining some of the shares. Given the above definition of investors' beliefs in the absence of signalling, the maximum revenue without signalling R_N would be

$$R_N = \frac{2n_m + \sum_{i\in\{0,1\}} [\beta_i + \gamma_i]}{1+r} \tag{2.33}$$

Clearly, $R_N < R_S$ iff condition 2.12 holds. Lastly, the state can affect the valuation of firm j by its choice of a_i if it chose $a_0 = a_1 = a$. In this case, given the result of proposition 2.2, the state revenues would be R_P:

$$R_P = \frac{\sum_{i\in\{0,1\}} [n + \beta_i + \gamma_i e^{-\frac{2n}{\gamma_g+\gamma_b}}]}{1+r} \tag{2.34}$$

It is easily shown that $R_S \geq R_P$, iff

$$\sum_{i\in\{g,b\}} \gamma_i e^{-\frac{n}{\gamma_i}} \geq (\gamma_g + \gamma_b) e^{-\frac{2n}{\gamma_g+\gamma_b}} \tag{2.35}$$

If $\gamma_g = \gamma_b$, condition 2.35 holds as an equality. The derivative of both sides of the above inequality with respect to γ_g is

$$(1-x)e^x \tag{2.36}$$

where x on the left hand side corresponds to $x_L = -\frac{n}{\gamma_g}$ and x on the right-hand-side corresponds to $x_R = -\frac{2n}{\gamma_g+\gamma_b}$. If $\gamma_g > \gamma_b > 0$ and $n > 0$ then $x_L > x_R$ and the derivative of the left hand side is always larger than the one on the right-hand-side. This implies that equation 2.35 always holds as a strict inequality for $\gamma_g > \gamma_b > 0$ so that $R_S > R_P$. □

2.6.2 Proof of Proposition 2.2

As has been shown above, the state would never choose $a_0 = a_1 = a$ if a separating equilibrium was feasible and condition 2.12 holds. The only case when a separating equilibrium is not feasible because the state cannot commit not to cheat is when condition 2.11 does not hold. Therefore there exists a pooling equilibrium whenever condition 2.11 does not hold and condition 2.12 holds. To find this equilibrium it is necessary to start from the FOC of the state under the restriction that a_0=a_1=a. In this case h_{10}=h_{00} =h_0 because investors can not differentiate which firm is which. Then the FOC is

$$2h_0 + 2a\frac{\partial h_0}{\partial a} + \frac{1-a}{1+r}(\frac{\partial V_{01}}{\partial a} + \frac{\partial V_{11}}{\partial a}) - \frac{1}{1+r}(V_{01} + V_{11}) = 0 \tag{2.37}$$

Given rational expectations it must be true that

$$h_0 = \frac{1}{2(1+r)}(V_{01} + V_{11}) \tag{2.38}$$

Equations 2.37, 2.38 and 3.15 then result in

$$\frac{\partial h_0}{\partial a} = \frac{\gamma_g + \gamma_b}{2(1+r)}(1 - \frac{1}{a}) \tag{2.39}$$

Integrating equation 2.39 results in

$$h_0 = \frac{-(\gamma_g + \gamma_b)\ln(a) + \sum\limits_{i\in\{g,b\}} \gamma_i a}{2(1+r)} + C \tag{2.40}$$

The constant C can be determined by further equilibrium considerations. Suppose in a signalling equilibrium the state sold everything at t_0. Then it must be the case that

$$h_0 = \frac{\sum\limits_{i\in\{g,b\}} \beta_i + \gamma_i a}{2(1+r)} \tag{2.41}$$

If it was smaller than the above value, competition among investors would drive the price up. If it was any larger, the state could sell firms for a price higher than their present value whenever the true n was 0. This cannot be the case in a fully revealing equilibrium. Therefore

$$C = \frac{\beta_g + \beta_b}{2(1+r)} \tag{2.42}$$

Equations 2.40, 2.42 and 2.37 result in 2.13.□

2.7 Appendix B

The above model is partly driven by $f(a)$. Concerning this function two questions remain. First, it needs to be clarified what exactly is to be understood by large potential corporate governance improvements and how they come about. In particular, a theoretical foundation is needed for why $f'(a)$ is positive for all a. Secondly, it needs to be clarified how the difference in the β's relate to the difference in the γ's. Only then would it become clear whether separating equilibria should be a common phenomenon.

Concerning the first issue, there are two different rationales for arguing that the size of the sell-off affects the value of the firm. *Holmstroem and Tirole (1993)* argue that public trading of a firm leads to a situation, where there is more information about the performance of the firm in its share-price than can be extracted from the firm's current or future profit data. Therefore, public trading of a firm makes it possible to write more efficient remuneration contracts for the firm's managers based on the additional information conveyed by shareprices. Furthermore, *Holmstroem and Tirole* show that a decrease in concentration of the shareholdings (i.e. by making the market of the shares more liquid) increases market incentives to collect information about the firm. Therefore, a dilution of ownership increases the value of the firm. In our case, this implies the following: If the state sold its stake not to one, but to a continuum of investors, the value of the firms would increase due to better market monitoring. However, it is far from clear whether this mechanism can work in the nascent security markets in transition economies. Therefore, the focus is on another source of corporate governance gains: the threat of a potential take-over of the firm by a corporate raider[15]. As was first put forward by *Grossmann and Hart (1980)*, there is a free-rider problem associated with this corporate governance mechanism: With atomistic shareholders a raider can buy its target only for a price that is equivalent or bigger than the target's value after the raider will have introduced all the improvements that it had identified. Given a costly take-over procedure, take-overs will therefore not happen and potential improvement will not be made. This problem can be overcome by a large shareholder, as has been proposed by *Shleifer and Vishny (1986)*: The large shareholder may be able to internalize enough of the gains to cover the costs of the take-over. Given, that the stake of the state (in general) goes to one private shareholder, this shareholder can

[15] Given that there already was a take-over attempt in Russia in the summer of 1995, it might well be that take-overs are going to play a non-negligible role in corporate governance in Russia.

overcome the free-rider problem. The larger the stake a of this private shareholder, the more of the gains he can internalize. This, in turn, makes it more likely that it is rational for him to buy the (50 - a)% necessary to implement an improvement he has discovered. In addition, this increases the intensity with which he searches for improvements. In particular, Shleifer and Vishny prove that the value of the firm rises with an increase in a. The only assumption still needed is then that the state itself is not as efficient in searching for improvements and implementing them as private investors.

In the *Shleifer and Vishny* framework, the question can also be answered, whether the model should have more time periods, because the corporate governance gains can presumably also be achieved after the state sold the rest of its shares at t_1. If this was the case, then the cost of keeping the shares is only due to the fact that the corporate governance gains need to be discounted for one more period. However, if (for exogenous reasons) a different investor will buy the rest of the shares at t_1, the corporate governance gains could be smaller than gains that would have been realized if everything was sold at t_1, even with a zero interest rate. The reason for this is that the size of the shareholding of the largest (outside) investor matters. Using the *Shleifer and Vishny* results and assuming that the values of potential improvements at firm i, Z_i, are distributed uniformly on $[0, Z_i^{max}]$, and that costs of participating in the auction are zero, the following relationship between a and the firm value is obtained:

$$f_i(a) = \frac{4I_i(a)Z_i^{max}a}{(1+2a)^2} \tag{2.43}$$

where $I(a)$ is a measure of the research intensity (which can be interpreted as the probability that an improvement that is distributed as described above in $[0, Z_i^{max}]$ is actually found). Assuming a quadratic cost function of undertaking research (such that the cost function is convex), the following explicit function for the research intensity is obtained.

$$I(a) = \frac{2Z_i^{max}a^2}{B(1+2a)^4}, \tag{2.44}$$

resulting in

$$f_i(a) = \frac{8(Z_i^{max})^2a^3}{B(1+2a)^4} \tag{2.45}$$

where $B > 0$ and $2BI$ is the marginal cost of doing research with intensity I. The firm value depends on a and $f\prime(a) > 0$ for all a. Furthermore, it depends positively on the maximum improvement that can be found by the investor. This is a natural interpretation of large potential corporate governance gains. Furthermore, it seems rather likely that the state has this information. In particular, it is not assumed that the state knows about an improvement, but cannot implement it itself. It is only assumed that the state knows the probability distribution of potential improvements.

It is to be noted, that the total state holding at t_0 cannot be normalized to one in this case, but needs to represent the percentage of the shares the state has not yet privatized. Only then can the variable 'a' be used in the same sense as in *Shleifer and Vishny* to denote the total amount the investor holds in the firm. The above derivation of $f(a)$ is only valid for $a < \frac{1}{2}$, since otherwise the investor has full control[16]. Linearising around a_f, the following expression is obtained:

$$f_i(a) = \frac{16(Z_i^{\max})^2 a_f^3(2a_f - 1)}{B(1+2a_f)^5} + \frac{8(Z_i^{\max})^2 a_f^3(3 - 2a_f)}{B(1+2a_f)^5} a. \qquad (2.46)$$

In this case a_f should be the ex-ante expected sell-off, which must be the same for both firms as the ex-ante probability for a firm to have a large $Z_i^{\max}$ is $\frac{1}{2}$. Then large γ's are associated with small β's because $2a_f - 1$ is negative. This means that the non-cheating condition 2.11 is rather likely to be true if the β's are interpreted as a result of the linearisation procedure.

[16] This fits the Russian reality quite well, where stakes sold in the second stage of privatisation are typically between 20% and 38% (see *Russian Economic Trends*). Furthermore, a fringe of small shareholders (as assumed in the *Shleifer and Vishny* model) exists as workers hold a large extent of the shares.

3. Shareholder Rights in Russia: An Empirical Investigation

3.1 Introduction

This chapter aims to analyse the factors that determine whether firms in a sample of 140 Russian firms choose to introduce shareholder rights in order to mitigate the agency problems between managers and shareholders. In terms of existing literature, this chapter should be seen in the context of *La Porta et al (1996)*. The authors have shown that the legal set-up matters with respect to the ownership arrangement of joint stock companies. Countries with relatively weak legal protection of share ownership tend to have more concentrated ownership structures. Russia presents a textbook case of a country where legal institutions are underdeveloped and where the enforcement of laws cannot be relied upon. It therefore provides an interesting case study.

Agency problems between new shareholders of privatised firms and management appear to be very serious in many transition economies. In particular, there is some evidence that management expropriate a substantial part of firms' profits. For the case of Russia, there is some questionnaire evidence provided by the Russian Barometer, that 46% of workers believed that management would take funds out of the firm (see *Rose*, 1995). More concretely, *Nash and Willer* (1995) observe that profits in the economy as recorded in the national accounts appear to be much larger than is shown in companies' accounts. This is consistent with the assumption that a substantial part of profits (but presumably also a part of wages) remain unrecorded.

The agency problem arises from "weaknesses" in corporate governance. According to most surveys, management remained in control of privatized firms, in spite of not being the formal owners. Outside shareholders rarely had any influence on management behaviour. For the case of Russia, see for example *Blasi and Shleifer (1996) or Klepach et al (1996)*[1]. This largely unchecked separation of ownership and control creates a considerable scope

[1] There is also some evidence from the 'New Russia Barometer' *(Rose, 1995)*. 30% of employees agreed with the statement that real power was kept by management, and 41% agreed somewhat. *Earle, Estrin and Leshchenko (1996)* found that management was by far the most influential unit in a firm, even in firms where

for moral hazard and makes it likely that a substantial part of profits are diverted by management. This raises the question of why this agency problem is not mitigated by a well functioning system of corporate governance. So far, the literature has answered this question by drawing attention to the privatisation process which resulted in rather dispersed ownership. In particular, *Boycko et al (1995)* show that in the case of Russia the privatisation process allocated considerable amounts of shares to insiders (workers and management). Some of the remaining shares were partly given away for free to the population (voucher-privatisation) and partly sold to outside blockholders. The residual shares are still held by the State. In general *Boycko et al* show that the amount allocated to outside blockholders was rather small. They argue that since the owners of small share packages have little incentive to collect costly information to monitor management, many firms are still effectively controlled by management. However, the authors also predict that this problem would be mitigated over time. As workers or the population sell their shares, outside blockholders with an incentive to monitor will grow in importance. Furthermore, by selling the remaining state-owned shares directly to outside blockholders, the power of management would also be curbed.

This chapter will give some evidence that blockholders now exist in many of the 140 largest Russian firms. The mean holding of the largest outside blockholder in this sample is 23% of share capital. However, even given such blockholders, the mechanism of corporate governance does not seem to be working optimally because property rights do not seem to be legally enforceable. This paper presents several indicators that are capturing some aspect of whether the property rights of shareholders are respected. The variation of these indicators across firms is very substantial. This variation implies that the management of a given firm can to some degree choose whether to honour shareholder rights or not. This is only possible if property rights are not legally enforceable, as otherwise all firms would be forced to honour shareholder rights[2]. For example, in October 1996 10% of the shares of Surgutneftegaz were issued and sold below market prices to the Surgut

outsiders had substantial share ownership. The influence of outside shareholders therefore seemed to have been limited in 1995.

[2] It is worth noting that these problems are not specific to Russia. The 1995 International Finance Corporation (IFC) Factbook of Emerging Markets lists only 5 out of the 26 emerging markets it covers as having investor protection of an internationally acceptable quality. It also singles out the Chinese equity market for having especially poor investor protection. While this chapter focuses on Russia in its empirical investigation, which had not been included in the last IFC ranking, the findings are relevant to other emerging markets as well.

Holding company, which is controlled by insiders[3]. On the other hand, the institutional shortcoming of non-enforceable property rights does not appear to be a problem in every firm. The data presented in this chapter does indicate that some firms start to honour shareholder rights, although it is only a minority among the 140 largest Russian firms (by sales) whose shares are traded on the over the counter market[4].

This chapter develops a simple model that aims to determine which firms choose to honour shareholder rights in an environment where property rights are not legally enforceable. The benefits of honouring shareholder rights are that new capital can be raised to fund new projects. But this is at the cost of reduced possibilities for management to expropriate profits. This model generates several hypotheses on what could drive the introduction of shareholder rights. In particular, firms where the moral hazard problem is smaller (i.e. potential expropriation is low) have low costs of introducing shareholder rights and are more likely to do so. Also, firms with larger investment needs are, *ceteris paribus*, more likely to introduce shareholder rights. It is also shown that large blockholders with the power to force managers to introduce shareholder rights may do so and thereby mitigate the management's expropriation rather than cooperate in this expropriation. The State might also force managers to introduce shareholder rights.

This model is tested with a (limited) data set. The key findings are the following: Shareholder rights (i.e. the dependant variable) are proxied by five different variables, which are all significantly positively correlated. To the extent that the amount that can be expropriated in a given firm is positively correlated with size, the model is confirmed since larger firms turn out to be more likely to honour shareholder rights. There is also some limited evidence that firms with a larger outside blockholder are more likely to honour shareholder rights and there is weak evidence that this is also true for the state as a blockholder. Investment needs, as proxied by different industry variables, are significant in some specifications. However, more shareholder friendly behaviour does not seem to be reflected in higher valuations of the firms' shares.

---

[3] While the share issue had been authorized by shareholders at the annual shareholders meeting, the price at which the sale took place might constitute a violation of the law on joint stock companies. This law lays out that new issues have to be sold at or above market prices. The Federal Securities Commission (FSC), the regulatory body for the Russian capital markets with ministerial rank, has examined the case and consequently an out-of-court settlement was reached where the shares were sold at a higher price, but still below the market price.

[4] These shares are not necessarily very liquid. Only for about 50 firms there is reliable shareprice information available. Shares in the other 80 firms are highly illiquid and only very few trades occur.

This chapter is organized as follows: Section 3.2 describes the model. Section 3.3 describes the (limited) data-set. Section 3.4 tests the hypothesis of section 3.2 and finally section 3.5 contains the conclusions.

3.2 Which Firms Honour Shareholder Rights ? A Simple Framework

Shareholder rights are modelled so as to prevent management from expropriating profits. This section derives two different but related models of the introduction of shareholder rights under different assumptions on the nature of the game played between management and outside blockholders in the absence of shareholder rights. The first section assumes that management has complete control over the firm in the absence of shareholder rights. The second section gives some bargaining power to outside blockholders. The only difference in the results will be that the size of outside blockholders is negatively correlated with the probability of the introduction of shareholder rights in the first case, and positively in the second.

3.2.1 Complete Management Control

ASSUMPTION 3.1: In the absence of shareholder rights management has complete control over the firm, irrespective of the size of its own stake in the firm, denoted by M.

ASSUMPTION 3.2: In the absence of shareholder rights management can expropriate a part of profits with a present value of b. This amount is a function of firm size, as measured by employment e: $b(e)$. Denote the value of the assets net of expropriation by $a(e)$.

If there were significant economies of scale in monitoring firms, larger firms would be more tightly observed and more often regulated by government institutions than small ones. The tax authorities, regulatory bodies, ministries or former ministries would be much more likely to scrutinize large firms than small ones[5]. This should make it harder for these firms to expropriate on a large scale. Furthermore, the punishment if caught stealing is likely to be higher for the large firms, because they are much more visible. It makes more sense to punish them severely to deter other firms from stealing. Therefore, the expected value of expropriation should decrease with size. On the other hand, it can be argued that larger firms operate in a more complex environment which increases the possibility to expropriate. Therefore, the empirical investigation should help to discover the correct sign of the derivative of b

[5] In 1996 the Russian State Tax Service created an extra unit to deal with the largest firms in an effort to improve tax compliance of large firms.

with respect to e. Apart from the possibility to steal, management also gets private benefits from running the company.

ASSUMPTION 3.3: Private benefits for management, c, are an increasing function of employment: $c(e)$, $c' > 0$.

With the introduction of shareholder rights, the game between management and outside blockholders changes as described by the following three assumptions.

ASSUMPTION 3.4: If shareholder rights are introduced, it is impossible to expropriate, i.e $b = 0, \forall e$.

With the introduction of shareholder rights, management gives certain rights to outside investors and as a result might lose control. This is more likely the larger the stake of the largest outside blockholder, denoted by L, and the smaller its own stake in the company, M.

ASSUMPTION 3.5: If shareholder rights were introduced, management loses its private benefits c with probability $p(M, L)$, where $\frac{\partial p(M,L)}{\partial M} < 0$ and $\frac{\partial p(M,L)}{\partial L} > 0$.

ASSUMPTION 3.6: Only if shareholder rights were introduced is it possible to obtain external finance for a project whose present value accruing to old shareholders is n.

While this assumption is a simplification, it captures the idea that only if shareholders have rights to affect control decisions in their interest, will they contribute funds. The same is likely to be the case for lenders. With respect to share-issues this chapter will provide some limited evidence for this assumption. With respect to lending decisions, see, for example, *EBRD* [6].

The objective for management is to maximize its expected return. In this set-up risk-neutral management compares the pay-offs with shareholder rights and without shareholder rights and therefore chooses to introduce shareholder rights, iff

$$E[Ma(e) + b(e) + c(e)|\Omega] \leq E\{M[a(e) + b(e)] + [1 - p(M, L)]c(e) + Mn|\Omega\} \tag{3.1}$$

[6] In the context of the examination of shareholder rights, it would be natural to interpret the outside finance as raised by equity issues. However, bond issues are possible as well. To some extent the argument above can be applied to bond issues. After all, firms that do not expropriate presumably find it easier to raise finance by bonds. In any case, there are at present no markets for corporate debt, but there is a reasonably liquid one for equities. This would facilitate equity issues compared to debt issues. Apart from tradable debt, there is the possibility to obtain loans. However, up to the present time, there have not been many significant long-term loans (see *Russian Economic Trends, Volume 1997.1)*.

where E denotes expectations, conditional on the information set of management of the firm, denoted by Ω. Without shareholder rights management obtains its legal share of profits that are not expropriated plus the profits it can expropriate, plus the private benefits from control. With shareholder rights it would obtain its legal share of total profits (i.e. profits that had not been expropriated and that had been expropriated in the absence of shareholder rights) plus the expected value of private benefits (now lower as there is some chance of management losing control) plus management's share of the new project.

This simplifies to

$$E[b(e)|\Omega] \leq E[\frac{Mn - p(M,L)c}{1-M}|\Omega] \quad (3.2)$$

It is straightforward to see how management's choice is influenced by the different parameters. The results are summarized in the following proposition:

PROPOSITION 3.1: Under Assumptions 3.1 to 3.6, shareholder friendly behaviour is more likely, the larger the gains of the new investment, n, and the larger the share of management, M. Shareholder friendly behaviour is less likely, the more can be stolen in a given firm, b, the larger the private benefits, c, and the larger the stake of the outside blockholder, L.

The intuition behind these comparative statics exercises is straightforward. The more profitable the new investment for the old shareholders and the less management loses by ceasing to expropriate profits, the more likely is it to introduce shareholder rights[7]. Also, the smaller the private benefits for management, which are endangered in case shareholder rights are introduced, the more likely management is to introduce shareholder rights. Lastly, with respect to ownership, the likelihood of shareholder friendly behaviour in the above model increases with the share owned by management and decreases with the share owned by the largest outside shareholder. This is the case for two reasons. First, the more management owns, the smaller is the perceived threat to its control. Therefore, management gains less from trying to discourage active participation of outside shareholders in shareholder meetings. Second, the more management owns, the smaller are the incentives to expropriate since it owns a larger part of the profits legally[8]. The argument assumes that the different layers of management that own shares collude and

[7] *Akamatsu (1995)* reports an example of the former mechanism at work. Alfa Capital, who had bought 25% of Bolshevik Biscuit Company in December 1992, was not permitted into the shareholders meeting. Subsequently Alfa Capital applied to a court, but without success. Finally, management allowed Alfa Capital into the meeting after it had promised to raise money to modernize the Bolshevik plant.

[8] In a sample of *Klepach et al (1996)* the firms with management as the largest blockholder are more likely to implement an "active survival" strategy than

act like one shareholder would. If instead they compete in stealing from the firm this effect is unlikely to be observed[9]. As regards employment, the effect is not clear. An additional argument on the potential impact of e are fixed costs to access capital markets. These fixed costs could deter smaller firms from aiming to tap these markets, which would reduce their incentives to implement shareholder friendly policies. However, the fact that the sample only includes firms that are relatively large, makes this argument rather unconvincing.

3.2.2 Limited Management Control

The above model relies on the assumption that management behaviour is completely unchecked. In reality, the freedom of management is likely to be restricted by outside blockholders. Even though privatisation very often resulted in handing out large parts of the shares to insiders, the data presented in this chapter shows that there are nevertheless quite a number of outside blockholders in many Russian enterprises. These outsiders can be banks, investment funds and brokerages, financial-industrial groups, non-financial firms or foreign firms.

ASSUMPTION 3.7: Outsiders succeed in introducing shareholder rights against the will of management with probability $q(L, M)$ which depends positively on the size of the largest outside blockholder and negatively on the size of the share ownership of management, i.e. $\frac{\partial q}{\partial L} > 0, \frac{\partial q}{\partial M} < 0$.

The bargaining power depends on the relative stakes of the two parties. However, instead of pressing for shareholder rights, outside blockholders could collude with management. This is possible, as in this set-up it is assumed that management can make side-payments to the blockholder. If the blockholder is a supplier, this could take the form of a profitable contract granted to the blockholder. It could also be done by a direct bribe management pays out of its stolen profits b. If they collude, a bargaining game is played on how to split b. Abstracting from the possibility of a change of management (that is of redistributing c) the fallback option for management in case the bargaining breaks down is

$$E\{a(e)M + c(e) + [1 - q(L, M)]b(e) + q(L, M)M(b(e) + n)|\Omega\} \qquad (3.3)$$

employee-, state- or outsider-controlled firms. To the extent that this strategy comprises raising new funds, this finding supports the notion that the more management owns, the more likely is it that shareholder rights are introduced.

[9] The very simple model above is static and cannot explain why a firm would switch from shareholder unfriendly to shareholder friendly behaviour. The principal mechanism I would like to suggest is that management buys up shares and an increase in M would then lead to a switch in behaviour. This mechanism will be modelled in the following chapter.

as it can continue to steal with probability q but will only receive the share M of b with probability $(1 - q)$. In case shareholder rights are introduced management will also receive its share of the pay-offs of the new project, Mn. The expected value of the fallback option of the outsider is

$$E[a(e)L + q(L, M)L(b(e) + n)|\ \bar{\Omega}] \tag{3.4}$$

where $\bar{\Omega}$ denotes the information set of the outsiders concerning the firm. They get share L of the non-expropriated profits in any case, and receive a part of the new project as well as of b with probability q. Assuming that $\Omega = \bar{\Omega}$, the total amount the two parties can bargain over is

$$E[a(e)(L + M) + b(e) + c(e)|\Omega] \tag{3.5}$$

Collusion is the preferred strategy whenever there is a surplus over the fallback strategies for the two parties. This is true since the Nash bargaining mechanism makes both players with positive bargaining power strictly better off than their fallback option. Therefore, the two parties will not collude iff

$$E[b(e)|\Omega] \leq E[\frac{(L + M)n}{1 - L - M}|\Omega], \tag{3.6}$$

which is (3.5)-(3.4)-(3.3). In this case shareholder rights will be introduced with probability $q(L, M)$.

In this set-up it is still the case that management might introduce shareholder rights without any outside pressure, just as analysed in the previous section. Therefore, equation 3.2 is to be taken account of in this set-up as well. This results in three regions with varying likelihood of shareholder rights being introduced[10].

In the figure point A is given by equation 3.2 and point B by equation 3.6. For firms with values of b between 0 and A, management introduces shareholder rights, just as in the case with 100% management control. Between points A and B, shareholder rights are introduced with probability $q(L, M)$, if the outsider succeeds in pushing for shareholder rights. For values of b above point B, no shareholder rights are introduced as the outside blockholder and management collude. In this variation of the set-up, the comparative statics are essentially the same as above. The only exception is the change with respect to the share of the outside blockholder, L. This leads to the following proposition.

PROPOSITION 3.2: Under assumptions 3.2 to 3.7 the larger the share of the outsider, the more likely is it that shareholder rights are introduced.

Between points A and B the likelihood rises as the outsider becomes stronger and can push for these rights. At the same time point B shifts to

[10] Again, this abstracts from threats to changes in private rents c. Furthermore, liquidity considerations are disregarded in this set-up.

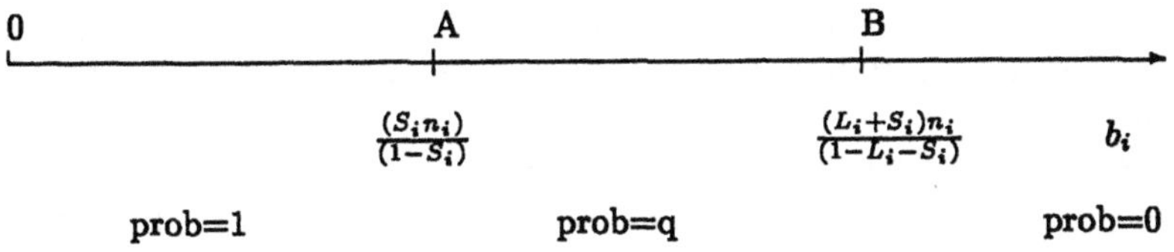

Fig. 3.1. The Effect of Stealing

the right, decreasing the region of collusion. This is true, as the benefit from taking advantage of the small outside shareholders decreases the larger the combined share of management and the large outsider[11]. This is the opposite of the case of 100% management control and an empirical investigation is necessary to see which of the two scenarios is more likely. If side payments were not possible, the likelihood of the introduction of shareholder rights in the area to the right of point B would be the same as between points A and B. Proposition 3.2 would therefore still hold.

3.2.3 Two Caveats

Two caveats have to be discussed in this context. First, ownership is in general not exogenous. Although this chapter represents very much an initial look at the ownership structures as they emerged from the privatisation programme, it is still possible that the size of the largest outside stake may be endogenous. In particular, as argued by *La Porta et al (1996),* concentration in outside ownership could act as a substitute for poor legal protection. If this was true, one would expect large shareholders to invest in firms that do not honour shareholder rights (to subsequently use their bargaining power to collude in stealing or to push for shareholder rights). Smaller shareholders, who have little bargaining power, are more likely to pick firms where management is committed to honour shareholder rights. Furthermore, it is only

[11] This is a similar prediction as the one made by *Shleifer and Vishny (1986)* who argue that cumulating shares reduces the free rider problem of monitoring management and therefore can make management more likely to maximize shareholders' wealth.

large shareholders, in a situation where shareholder rights are not honoured and collusion does not take place, who have an incentive to increase their stake L. This is true because the value of their existing shares increases with q, which is a positive function of L. Under this scenario the size of the small outside blockholding should be associated with relatively high levels of shareholder protection, just as in the case when the management controls the firm exclusively[12].

Second, apart from outside private blockholders, the State could play a role in controlling management. It is an important feature of large Russian enterprises that the State still holds substantial blocks of shares in many of them even after they have been privatised[13]. It has been asserted that the state does not in general use the control rights attached to the shares or is implicitly colluding with management (*Frydman et al, 1996*). However, it could be that this is only the case with respect to participation in strategic decisions, where the last decade has taught the State that it has no comparative advantage. It would seem more likely that the State does use its voting rights to press for the implementation of shareholder rights. This can be expected because the state is planning to sell-off its remaining stakes in the near future and should therefore be interested in higher shareprices. This commitment makes it different from the type of private outside blockholder who invests in the company for the long run. Apart from these private incentives as an owner, the State also has an interest to promote better corporate governance to increase the likelihood of successful restructuring. For this to happen a mechanism to re-allocate control rights is necessary, one of which could be the stockmarket. This possibility increases incentives for the state to push for shareholder friendly behaviour. As a matter of fact, the activities of the Federal Securities Commission (FSC) give some credibility to the hypothesis that the state recognizes its interest in promoting shareholder rights. More specifically, the government passed a resolution in February 1995 under which it will not provide any budgetary funds to companies which violate shareholder rights. While it is clear that enforcement of this legislation is difficult through the legal system, it seems possible that directors elected to the boards to represent the State are better positioned to influence management's decisions in

[12] If shareholder unfriendly management could prevent shareholders from increasing their stakes, this could lead to the opposite bias. However, this crudest form of violation seems to have given way to more subtle ones, e.g. not disclosing information etc. Also, there exists in general a free float of shares for the firms in the sample, which could be bought up. See *Brunswick Brokerage*, 1996 *Equity Report*.

[13] This has been described in more detail in chapter 2.

this respect[14]. On the other hand, if the State has other objectives like, for example, avoiding unemployment, it is unlikely that it would push for shareholder rights[15]. This is true as outside shareholders are in general more likely to restructure the enterprises actively.

3.3 The Data

3.3.1 The Dependent Variables: Shareholder Rights Indicators

Shareholder friendliness of management is difficult to measure, as it covers many aspects of management behaviour, only part of which can be directly observed by the econometrician. In this section, I present first some evidence about the importance of control rights of shares. Then several different indicators for measuring shareholder rights with respect to control rights as well as with respect to income rights are proposed, together with some institutional background to justify them. Subsequently, data is presented for the 140 largest traded Russian open joint stock companies. It is shown that the indicators for control rights are significantly positively correlated, which gives some evidence that they all might be valid measures of the underlying shareholder friendliness.

Shares give two different rights to its owners: rights of control and income-rights[16]. During transition, the more important feature of shares is arguably the control rights since the majority of privatized enterprises are in need of severe restructuring. Then, control rights matter even more than during 'normal' times because many long-term strategic decisions, that can involve substantial sunk costs, have to be made. Furthermore, to the extent that privatisation has not resulted in an allocation of control rights that facilitates restructuring, this shortcoming can be mitigated in the secondary market. At the same time, income of firms is in many cases relatively low during transition, but expected to grow fast, such that income rights during the first years are of relatively little importance. This is reflected in the discount preference shares are traded at (table 3.1). This table shows the premium of ordinary shares over preference shares over time for some of the most liquid Russian companies, for which data are available. Preference shares have been

[14] In early 1998 the government used its shares to elect a reformer to the post of general manager of UES, the electricity monopoly.

[15] See, for example, *Shleifer and Vishny (1994)*. The authors show that public enterprises can be encouraged by politicians subject to pressure from interest groups, such as labour unions, to employ too many people.

[16] For one of the earliest manifestations of this idea see, for example, *Grossman and Hart (1980)*.

issued for free to employees by the firms that chose option 1 of privatisation (which roughly 25% did)[17]. These shares amount up to 25% of chartered capital. They have no voting rights attached but are in general guaranteed preferential treatment with respect to dividend payments. The details of this preferential treatment vary across firms and are laid down in the corporate charters. Most of these charters state that 10% of after tax profits, or the equivalent to the dividend on ordinaries, whichever is greater, have to be paid out as dividends to holders of preference shares.

Table 3.1. Premia of Ordinary Shares over Preference Shares as Percentage of Ordinary Share Price

Date	Rostelekom	UES	LUKOil	Surgut-neftegaz	Norilsk Nickel	Noyabrsk-neftegaz
2.10.95	95	85	88	87	62	86
10.1.96	93	68	83	82	57	86
1.4.96	68	62	70	67	29	72
3.7.96	56	74	65	78	62	69
26.9.96	41	46	40	49	50	49

Source: Prema-Invest

However, there are two other reasons for the discount the preference shares are trading at, apart from the missing voting rights. They are in general less liquid (see *Rinaco Plus research report R+, 1997*). Investors would therefore require a premium to be compensated for this illiquidity. However, liquidity would have been very likely to increase over time, as workers would be allowed to sell their shares. This should have been anticipated by rational investors. It seems unlikely that investors would have priced preferred shares at only 5% to 38% (depending on firm) of the value of the ordinary share in October 1995 because of only a *temporarily* reduced liquidity. The importance of the voting right is therefore likely to have played some part. Furthermore, as liquidity increased over time (see *Rinaco Plus research report R+, 1997*) the premium did not fully disappear but remained very substantial.

Second, the discount could also be related to a risk that preference shares are going to be swapped into ordinaries at unfavourable rates. However, holder of preference shares have the right to vote on these matters. As a swap would necessitate a change in the corporate charter which requires a 75% majority, this risk is rather small given that preference shares amount to

[17] The privatization process in Russia allowed for 3 different options to privatize a firm which differ by how much (and what type) of the shares are allocated to insiders.

25% of charter capital. The risk is therefore mainly relevant if management is in effect not bound by the corporate charter[18].

A discount of around 40% to 50% in Russia compares with much smaller discounts in the US (5%) but is similar in size to that found in Israel (31%) and Italy (45%). The latter two countries have much weaker protection of investors than the USA. This would also point towards the importance to shareholders to participate actively in shareholder meetings and the management of the company, in order to protect their investment in countries with weak legal enforcement mechanisms like Russia or Italy[19].

As income rights of equities are not fully codified in commercial law (it is in the nature of the equity contract that dividend payments cannot be enforced by a court), problems related to the difficulty of enforcing shareholder rights in Russia are mostly related to the control rights of shares. To examine the extent to which managers honour control rights of shares this chapter focuses on: whether American Depository Receipts (ADRs) or similar instruments were issued, the independence of shareholder registries and the provision of information to shareholders. In particular, five indicators, denoted by I_1 to I_5 are introduced. These are represented as the five columns in the matrix $I_{(140\times5)}$.

The first variable to proxy for shareholder friendliness, I_1, is a dummy variable on whether ADRs, Global Depository Receipts (GDRs) or Russian Depository Certificates (RDCs) have been issued. ADRs are certificates sold at an American securities exchange, denominated in USD, that are backed by shares that are held in custody in Russia. GDRs are similar to ADRs, but traded at stock exchanges outside the US. RDCs are also very similar certificates backed by Russian shares, held in custody by ING bank of the Netherlands. The buyers of these instruments are allowed to exercise the voting rights of the underlying share. An issue of ADRs, for example, indicates that management does honour shareholder rights to the extent that the costs of violating them increases if ADRs are outstanding. Theoretically, this seems

[18] The other striking feature of Table 3.1 is the large decrease of the premium of ordinary shares over preference shares over time. While this change is not directly relevant for the argument made in this chapter, this could have been the result of three different developments. First, as mentioned above, the increasing liquidity of preference shares reduced the premium of ordinary shares over preference shares. Second, it could have been the case that the differential in dividends between preference shares and ordinary shares grew over time. If, for example, dividends on ordinary shares fell strongly as firms were less profitable, but dividends on preference shares fell by less due to the statutes of the firm, this could also explain the observation in Table 3.1. However, this has not been the case for all the firms. For example, in the case of Rostelekom as well as in the case of Norilsk Nickel, the differential in dividends actually fell between 1996 and 1995. Lastly, Table 3.1 is consistent with a decrease of the value of the voting right over time, as firms start to honour shareholder rights to a larger extent and regulatory progress is made

[19] See, for example, *Levy (1982)* or *Zingales (1994)*.

plausible, as outstanding ADRs increase the likelihood that stealing profits is detected, as well as the likelihood of subsequent punishment. This is true as violations become more visible since the financial press covers them more thoroughly. This, in turn, is likely to increase the political pressure on management to undo or prevent such violations. The reason for this is that the Government might fear spill-over effects, that could damage the reputation of all Russian firms or even the reputation of the sovereign as a borrower[20]. For the case of Hong Kong, *Cheung and Shum (1995)* provide some empirical evidence on the reduction of risk associated with international stock listings. The authors examine events which increase the risk for the Hong Kong stockmarket but find that only the shares that are listed only in Hong Kong display a significant increase in their betas after the event, whereas shares listed in addition on the London Stock Exchange do not on average change their risk characteristics significantly. By January 1996, 10% of the sampled firms had issued one of these instruments. Issuance of ADRs are positively correlated with the other measures of shareholders' (control) rights.

The second aspect of shareholder friendly behaviour covered in this chapter is the openness with respect to information, covered by two variables; the survey measure I_2, and a dummy variable whether a firm has hired an international accounting company to do its accounts, I_5[21]. I_2 is the result of a survey by 'Agenstvo Konsultii i Marketing' (AK and M), who asked 308 participants in the survey to name up to 5 firms that were particularly open about disclosing information to investors (in order of openness). This survey was carried out in Q1 1996. The answers were then used to calculate the index[22].

The provision of information on the company to shareholders is an important part of shareholder rights. Information is necessary to evaluate the performance of management and to use the control rights of the shares in exercising corporate governance in a meaningful way. The importance of this point is stressed by a presidential decree of March 1996 which lays out a comprehensive programme on investors' and shareholders' rights and demands

[20] In an interview in the *Moscow Times* (16.11.96), management of Surgutneftegaz stated that 'competent analysts should have guessed that we were going to do this (the dilution) before the ADR issue (which is planned for later this year) because later it would be more difficult and more trouble'.

[21] The variable measures whether accounts have been done by Western accounting firms, not whether the firm has accounts published according to international accounting standards. While it does at times happen that these firms are asked to produce Russian style accounts, this seems to be quite rare. Furthermore, even if this is the case, it still signals that management is comparatively shareholder-friendly, as accounts checked by a Western accounting firm with a reputation to lose are likely to be more reliable than the ones provided by a Russian firm.

[22] steps of 5) implying that the final rating would be between 0 and 9,240. In response to this question, 222 companies were mentioned.

higher disclosure requirements for firms[23]. The recent struggle between outside investors, controlling 40% of the Novolipetsk Metallurgical Kombinat, and a management which refused to provide meaningful financial statements to the investors illustrates the problems inherent in this area[24]. I_5 is of importance as Russian accounting is still based on the necessities of a state economy and consequently does not provide information that helps to evaluate firms in a market environment. By January 1996 24% of the firms in the sample had (at least a partial) audit done by a international accounting firm. In September 1996, the government decided to grant tax reductions for firms that would adopt these international accounting principles[25]. I_2 and I_5 are significantly positively correlated (see table 3.2)[26].

Turning now to the independence of shareholder registries, there are two different variables; survey data measures the ease of transferability of shares, I_4, and a dummy variable measures whether the share-registries are licensed by the FSC, I_3. I_4 is based on a survey carried out by AK and M in Q1 1996. In this survey, 308 participants in the Russian stock market (150 Moscow firms and 158 regional firms) were asked to name up to 5 companies for which they found it particularly easy to transfer the ownership of stock (in order of convenience)[27].

The institutional background is the following: The issue of the reliability of share registries was historically the first concern of foreign investors with respect to shareholder rights. In particular, several well publicized instances occurred during 1994 and 1995, where management manipulated share registries or refused to register new shareholders[28]. Since share registries are the only proof of share-ownership in Russia this amounted in effect to negating property rights of outside investors. Subsequently, several steps were taken to mitigate this problem: a presidential decree was introduced in 1995 which

---

[23] In addition, the law on the securities market, which came into effect in April 1996, details disclosure requirements for the case of the issue of new securities.

[24] See *Financial Times*, of 21.2.1997. While outside investors have recently won a court victory against management, the court decision has not been implemented as of yet.

[25] See *MoscowTimes*, September 18, 1996. As this policy has been announced after the data on international accounting standards has been collected, it is unlikely to have affected the choice of accounting rules in the sample.

[26] The issue of an insufficient provision of information is also relevant in other countries. The *IFC Emerging Markets Handbook* lists only 8 out of the 26 markets it covers as meeting accounting standards of an internationally acceptable quality. China and Indonesia have especially poor accounting standards. In Jordan there are not even interim financial disclosure requirements implemented.

[27] Since another question in the survey related more directly to the liquidity of the share, this question is likely to pick up mainly legal aspects and differences in transaction costs of re-registering shares. These, in turn, can be directly controlled by management

[28] For example, in 1994 the director of the Krasnoyarsk Aluminium Factory cancelled out a 20% shareholding of a British metal firm. However, this shareholding was subsequently reinstated due to political pressure on management.

makes independent share-registries for firms with more than 1,000 employees obligatory. Based on this decree the FSC issued interim regulations on the maintenance of share registers in July 1995. These regulations determine how lawful entries into the share registries are to be made and also introduced a liability of the registrar for any improper performance of its duties. Furthermore, the regulations stipulate that share registries need to obtain a licence from the FSC. By August 30th, 1996, licences to 104 share registries in 49 regions have been granted. By September 1996, 17% of the largest 140 Russian firms had their shares registered by a licensed share registry. As is to be expected, the I_4 and I_3 are significantly positively correlated (see table 3.2). This seems to indicate that the licensing procedure of the FSC is effective in the sense that licensed registries seem to involve lower risk of improper handling of entries than unregistered ones.

With respect to income rights, the dividend policy for ordinary shares of firms is analysed[29]. The average dividend payout ratio announced in 1995 (for the fiscal year of 1994) was 2.5% of profits, with a minimum of 0% and maximum of 76%. For 1994 unfortunately there exists only a dummy variable for whether a dividend payment was announced (for the fiscal year of 1993). Because there was no liquid market for many of the shares in the sample, there are often no meaningful shareprices available. Therefore this chapter uses the payout-ratio ('Div') instead of dividend yields.

Table 3.2. Correlation of Indicators of Shareholder Rights

	IAS	ADR	Disclosure	Div	Licence	Transfer
IAS	1.000	0.345	0.326	-0.001	0.233	0.301
		(0.000)	(0.000)	(0.986)	(0.005)	(0.000)
ADR		1.000	0.577	0.122	0.274	0.488
			(0.000)	(0.150)	(0.001)	(0.000)
Disclosure			1.000	0.139	0.314	0.883
				(0.101)	(0.000)	(0.000)
Div				1.000	0.047	0.065
					(0.579)	(0.443)
Licence					1.000	0.350
						(0.000)
Transfer						1.000

p-values in brackets

[29] In this context, it is important to focus on dividends paid on ordinary shares and not on preference shares. This is true as during the privatization process preference shares were only issued to employees, not to any outsiders. Subsequent trading in these shares was very limited as workers were obliged to keep these shares for three years after privatization. Therefore, dividends on preference shares mainly reflect payments to insiders and do not indicate good behaviour with respect to outside shareholders.

All indicators relating to control rights of shares are significantly positively correlated. This gives some evidence that the underlying management behaviour with respect to outside shareholders is captured at least to some extent by these variables. However, as some of the variables are binary the coefficient of correlation is not necessarily the most appropriate statistic. In the appendix alternative measures for the correlation of the binary variables are provided. It is noteworthy that the dividend yield is not significantly positively correlated with the other indicators, although dividends could in general be a used to signal that shareholder rights are honoured[30]. This could indicate that the agency costs of outside finance are so large in Russia, that they more than outweigh the benefits of signalling the high quality of management[31].

3.3.2 Independent Variables

As opposed to the enterprise surveys carried out by the World Bank and by *Blasi and Shleifer (1996)*, who use data directly collected from the firms, this chapter analyses data on enterprises collected by brokerages and financial information services. Therefore, all the firms in the sample are organized as open joint stock companies. Furthermore, the data set comprises only information on the largest Russian firms (by sales), as the interest of investors is naturally highest in these firms. This makes this study complementary to the ones mentioned above, which focus mainly on small and medium sized firms. Furthermore, the focus on large firms should give the study some macroeconomic relevance, as the firms in the sample represent a significant amount of the total industrial workforce (27%). Given that data is collected in a transition economy the quality of the data might be questioned. In particular, it is unclear to what extent managers reveal information truthfully. It seems likely that differences in the quality of data between direct sampling and using information of brokerages are slight, as these institutions obtain their information by visiting the enterprise and interviewing management as well. Since brokerages are likely to have other sources of information on these firms, it could be the case that they find it easier to cross-check the data and improve its reliability. For example, information on the ownership structure of a firm can be cross-checked by observing its annual shareholders' meeting - which brokerages do to some extent. Furthermore, these brokerages have access to the products of financial information providers such as *Skatepress* and *Dun and Bradstreet*, which also interview companies and their management. Nevertheless, it is possible that some outside blockholdings are omitted in the data used. This problem should be more important for relatively small

[30] Formally, a dividend signaling model along the lines of *Ross (1977)* or *Bhattarchaya (1979)* could be constructed to fit this case. The model developed in chapter 4 generates similar predictions.

[31] This is consistent with *Mayer (1989)* who argues that in environments where external intervention is costly internal finance will dominate.

stakes, as these shareholdings are not necessarily disclosed during the annual meeting. Therefore, in the regression analysis I focus on the stake of the largest outside blockholder, where omissions should be less significant. The sample of this chapter was constructed by merging data from different sources into one dataset. Since the data originates from three different sources, *Brunswick Brokerage, Renaissance Capital* and *Troika Dialog*, it is possible that different series have different numbers of observations.

The sample used contains 140 firms with overall employment of 3.9 million. The mean employment is 25,300. The firms are concentrated in the following industries: communications, electricity, metallurgy, transport as well as oil[32]. The majority of firms are registered in Moscow, but the location of firms varies considerably. The clustering of firms in the Moscow area does not necessarily imply a regional bias, since a firm whose production facilities are all located in Siberia could get registered in Moscow[33].

Ownership data is given as of the end of January 1996. The average number of outside blockholders is 1.7, the median is 1.0. Blockholders are defined as institutions or individuals that hold more than 5% of the outstanding shares of a firm. These blockholders hold together on average 29.7% of the shares, with a median of 27.6. The largest of the blockholders holds on average 23.0 %, the median being 20% of a firm's equity. In 17% of firms, no outside blockholder is reported. These values are similar to the ones found by the *Blasi and Shleifer* survey (BSS) of medium sized firms (see table 3.3). They report for the end of 1995 an average stake of outsiders of 31.2%. However, the composition of outside blockholders is very different in the two samples. The following numbers report the average of the largest owner of a given type in a given firm[34]: The outside owner with the largest average stake were holding-companies and officially registered financial-industrial groups (FIGs) with an average equity holding of 11.4%. The second largest outside stake is held by non-financial firms, which hold on average 6.7% of outstanding shares. Investment funds (including brokerages) have the same average stake as banks (3.5%). Lastly, foreign financial firms own an average stake of 2.1% of the firms in the sample[35]. However, the distribution is highly uneven. The median for all these ownership classes is 0%, i.e. in more than 50% of firms, the given type of investor does not own any shares. The ownership structure

[32] For a detailed breakdown by industry see the appendix.

[33] To some extent it can even be argued that it is a sign of shareholder friendly behaviour to register a firm in Moscow, as outside shareholders might find it easier to attend the annual meeting. Therefore, it is not advisable to control for the region in which the firm is registered when running the regressions that are supposed to explain whether shareholder rights are honoured.

[34] This means, that if two investment funds have a block in a given company, the average includes only the block held by the larger of the two.

[35] It should be noted that January 1996 was a point where foreign involvement in the Russian equity market was at its lowest point this year. Therefore, one would expect much higher values for foreign ownership in late 1996.

by industry is given in the Appendix. Compared to BSS, where holding companies or FIGs own on average 4.9%, this sample has a much higher average ownership by this type of institution and a much lower ownership by Russian commercial firms.

Apart from outside owners, there are also pronounced differences in the stake the State still holds in these firms, denoted by '*State*'. In my sample, the average stake amounts to 13%, as opposed to 9% in BSS. In both cases the median is 0, pointing once more to the concentration of stakes. These numbers also could imply that the state is more actively involved in the management of the larger firms.

Table 3.3. Ownership of Russian Firms

	This Sample	BSS
Sample Size	140	185
Date	Jan-96	Q4-95
Mean Employment	25,300	2,444
Mean number of outside blockholders	1.7	NA
Mean holding of outside blockholders	29.7	31.0
Mean holding of largest blockholder	23.0	NA
of which		
Holdings or FIGs	11.4	2.6
Non-financial firms	6.7	14.6
Investment Funds	3.5	4.9
Banks	3.5	2.0
Foreign financial firms	2.1	0.0
State	13.0	9.0

There is unfortunately no data available covering insider ownership. Furthermore, there is no obvious proxy for this variable. This is a clear deficiency of my dataset. However, to the extent that this chapter provides an initial look at ownership structures as they resulted from privatisation, this omission should not bias the results. In particular, the first stage of privatisation should have resulted in a broadly similar extent of management ownership in the different firms. While the purchase of additional shares by management can be expected to take place over time, this development is likely to be slowed down to the extent that management is wealth constrained. This is in line with data reported by *Blasi et al*, who show that the increase in management shareholding has so far been slow. The dynamic aspects of insider ownership are examined in more detail in the following chapter.

Some of the variables in the simple model outlined above are not directly observable. Ideally, in order to capture the benefits from raising capital, n, investment needs would need to be observed directly, for example by an estimate of the change in demand for the products of a particular firm as well as the replacement needs with respect to existing capital. In this chapter industry dummies are used to capture n. In particular, a dummy for the communications industry ('Comm'); for the electricity industry ('Electricity'); for the oil and gas industry ('Oil'), for the metal industry ('Metal') and for transportation ('Transport') are used[36]. The set of industry dummies is denoted by D. One approach to determine which industries have particularly high investment needs would be to focus on replacement needs. Assuming that the physical assets of all firms have to be replaced to a similar extent, replacement needs of fixed capital depend on the percentage of fixed assets on the balance sheet. While it can be shown that industry dummies pick up significant differences in the percentage of fixed assets on the balance sheet (with the communications industry having the highest ratio of fixed assets and the metal industry the lowest one), the fact that these ratios are taken from the firm's Russian financial accounts, which cannot be compared to the Western equivalent, implies that those figures should only be used with extreme caution. Instead, the table below focuses on the cumulative change in production over the period between 1995 and 1990, the beginning of the transition. Assuming that supply has been largely fixed over this period (or has fallen to a similar extent) as investment during the first years of transition was very low (see ***Russian Economic Trends***), the majority of changes in prices and quantities is presumably due to changes in demand. If this was true, the industries where output fell the least and prices (deflated by the industrial price index) rose the most, are the ones where demand dropped the least. These should be the industries with the highest investment needs in order to replace a sufficient amount of the depreciated assets in order to meet this demand. Under these assumptions table 3.4 indicates that the communications industry and the electricity industry are the industries with the highest investment needs, whereas the metal industry has the lowest investment needs[37].

While this approach does not allow for firm specific differences in investment needs, there does not seem to be an obvious way around this problem without having to rely on accounting records drawn up according to Russian accounting standards. However, it could be argued that the large Russian firms are more homogenous than their Western counterparts. This could be

[36] A list of all variables used in this chapter is attached in the appendix.

[37] It is indeed plausible that the investment needs in the communications industry are particularly high as demand for communications services multiplied with the change of the economic system in Russia. It is also worth noting that the first (and to date only) Russian firm to issue a level 3 ADR was the telecom provider Vimplecom.

Table 3.4. Fall in Output and Change in Prices by Industry

Industry	Change in Price*	Change in Output**
Comm	267	+350***
Electricity	239	-20
Transport****	164	-40
Oil	191	-35
Metal	117	-45

Source: Goskomstat
* change in prices between end 1990 and end 1995, deflated by the PPI,
** change in real output between 1990 and 1995,
*** international telephone calls,
**** cargo

true as the firms in the same industry were set-up by the same planning agency which could imply that they have similar investment needs.

3.4 Testing the Hypotheses

The main aim of this section is to test the hypotheses of proposition 3.1 and proposition 3.2, using the limited dataset described in the previous section. This is implemented with the following set of regressions (the 'shareholder rights' regressions):

$$\bar{I}= C + \alpha_1 D + \alpha_2 e + \alpha_3 State + \alpha_4 L + \varepsilon \tag{3.7}$$

where C is a constant, $\bar{I}$ is a vector of the five different indicators with respect to control rights of shareholders, D is the vector containing five industry dummies (and α_1 consequently (5×1) vector) and ε is assumed to be an identical and independently distributed (iid) error term. As the data seems to indicate that the relationship with respect to L is not linear, L^2 is also added to give a second specification.

$$\bar{I}= C + \alpha_1 D + \alpha_2 e + \alpha_3 State + \alpha_4 L + \alpha_5 L^2 + \upsilon \tag{3.8}$$

where υ is assumed to be iid. As there are no instruments available for L OLS regressions are run under the assumption that the independent variables, and in particular L, are all exogenous. However, the equation is also run without L in a third specification to avoid the problem that the results are driven by a potential endogeneity of the largest outside stake.

$$\bar{I}= C + \alpha_1 D + \alpha_2 e + \alpha_3 State + \epsilon \tag{3.9}$$

Again, ϵ is assumed to be iid distributed. OLS is used for the estimation of I_2 and I_4 and Probit for estimation of I_1, I_3 and I_5, the binary variables.

Subsequently, this section tests the strong assumption 3.6. In particular, it had been assumed that firms can only raise new capital if they honour shareholder rights. This section gives some evidence that the number of share issues is indeed positively correlated with the five indicators of shareholder rights. It then tests whether the p/e ratio is higher in firms that honour shareholder rights. If this is true, this would also give some evidence for assumption 3.6, as it would imply that management can raise finance more cheaply by issuing shares. Such a result would be in the spirit of assumption 3.6. To implement this test I use the *Gordon and Shapiro (1956)* growth model. According to this model the p/e ratio (*PE*) can be expressed as

$$PE = \frac{Div}{r - g} \tag{3.10}$$

where *Div* is the dividend pay-out ratio, r is the required rate of return and g is the growth rate of the firms' profits. The required rate of return, r, in the framework of the CAPM (in its ex-post empirically testable form) would be

$$r = \gamma + \beta r_m + \eta \tag{3.11}$$

where γ in the *Sharpe-Lintner* framework would be $(1 - \beta)r_f$, where r_f is the risk free rate of return, β is the beta of the share, i.e. the covariance between the return of the market portfolio and the return of the share divided by the variance of the return on the market portfolio and r_m is the return of the market portfolio. This *Gordon and Shapiro* model together with the CAPM has, for example, been tested over a cross-section of countries by *Kim and Koveos* (1994). However, the model in section 3.2 implies that the cost of capital r depends also on whether shareholder rights are honoured:

$$r = r(\beta, z_1) \tag{3.12}$$

where the $\frac{\partial r}{\partial \beta} > 0$ and $\frac{\partial r}{\partial z_1} < 0$. A higher degree of shareholder friendliness should lower the cost of capital. To capture differences in expected future growth industry dummies are used. This is consistent with the use of industry dummies as proxies for investment needs, at least under the assumption that the old capital stock has to be replaced to a similar extent in all firms. Equations 3.10, 3.11 and 3.12 result in the following regression for the augmented *Gordon and Shapiro* model (the 'PE' regression):

$$PE = \gamma_1 z_1 + \gamma_2 D + \gamma_3 Div + \gamma_4 \beta + \xi \tag{3.13}$$

where ξ is the iid disturbance term. From the above analysis, the hypothesis for the augmented *Gordon and Shapiro* model would be the following:

PROPOSITION 3.3: In regression 3.13 $\gamma_1 > 0, \gamma_3 > 0, \gamma_4 < 0$

The regressions 3.7 and 3.13 (or 3.9 and 3.13 respectively) form a system of equations as the dependent variable in regression 3.7 is an independent variable in regression 3.13. The system is a recursive one. This allows to estimate equation 3.13 by two stage least squares, using *State*, L and e as instruments. Given the limited number of instruments and the high positive correlation among the I_1 to I_5 an index z_1 is constructed to reduce the problem of multi-collinearity. The index is constructed by applying the method of principal components. The use of principal components is an attempt to extract from a set of collinear variables a small number of variables that account for most or all of the variation in the set of variables (for details see appendix). The largest weight is given to I_2 (49%), followed by I_4 (35%), I_1 (12%), I_5 (8%) and I_3 (7%).

Before this system is estimated, two questions need to be raised: First, should PE also be a variable on the right hand side of equation 3.7 ? It could be argued that to the extent that the industry dummies do not pick up the true investment needs of the firms, high investment needs might be reflected in a higher p/e ratio. This approach is only used in the appendix. This is partly dictated by the data. As there are only 66 observations of the p/e ratio and only 32 stocks for which there is sufficient price data to attempt to estimate β, because many of the shares were very illiquid and therefore there is no meaningful price data for them, the sample would be reduced by more than 75% if the p/e ratio was included. Nevertheless, to show that PE is not significant, regressions including this variable on the right hand side are reported in the appendix, using 3SLS. This is done for the system of equation containing I_2, I_4 and PE as the endogenous variables. A further system of equations also including I_1, I_3 or I_5 as endogenous variables has not been constructed as the order condition would indicate that the number of instrumental variables would be insufficient. Furthermore, a system of equations containing endogenous binary variables as well as non-binary variables is not straight-forward to estimate, unless strong assumptions on the nature of the binary variables are made. The results from estimating both systems of equations imply that not much would be gained by making PE endogenous. In particular, PE is insignificant at the 10% level in the 3SLS regressions. Few variables remain significant in those regressions, presumably partly due to the sharply lower number of observations, but potentially also due to the correlation structure between PE and some of the exogenous variables. However, employment remains significant in most of the specifications and the variable 'State' is significant at the 10% in the I_4 regression. A more fundamental reason for not including PE (which also casts some doubt over the PE regressions estimated below) is that earnings are taken from the Russian accounts. Therefore, they have to be interpreted with extreme caution and are not easily comparable with the Western concept of earnings (see *Coopers and Lybrand, 1996*). Lastly, as argued above, large Russian firms in a given industry are likely to be more homogenous than their Western counterparts which could imply that firm level variation in investment needs is smaller than in the West.

Second, the question remains whether the index z_1 should be used as a right-hand-side variable in equation 3.13 or whether one should allow the data to determine the weights individually. Using the index has two advantages. First, the number of instruments is limited: 'State', 'L' and 'e'. This means that the system is not identified by the order condition if all five variables are put into equation 3.13. One would then have to make a subjective choice of which three variables to use. Second, using all five indicators creates a very substantial problem of multicollinearity. Therefore, the paper uses the index when estimating equation 3.13. However, this chapter will also provide the results when using two subsets of individual indicators.

As White tests indicated that the hypothesis of non-heteroskedasticity has to be rejected at the 5% level for these regressions, the OLS as well as the probit regressions were run with a robust variance-covariance matrix. As F tests indicate that the relationship with respect to L is non-linear, the following table (3.5) reports the estimation of 3.8. The estimation of 3.7 is reported in the appendix.

The I_2 regression, as reported in the first column of table 3.5, has an adjusted R^2 of 0.26 and is significant at the 5% level. Employment 'e' has a positive coefficient which is significant at the 1% level. Formally, I cannot distinguish whether this is due to fixed costs of entering the capital market or due to the higher expected value of expropriation in small firms. However, the latter argument is more plausible, as even the smaller firms in the sample are likely to have investment needs that are large enough to make the fixed costs of equity issues negligible. Then the derivative of b with respect to e would be positive. There is no evidence that expropriation in larger firms is facilitated due to the more complex environment. Furthermore, if private benefits to management of running the firm, c, are positively correlated with 'e', they are more than outweighed by the expropriation.

The variable 'State' has a positive coefficient, which is, however, not significant at the 10% level. The hypothesis that the State hinders the introduction of shareholder rights because it wants to avoid restructuring for exogenous reasons is clearly not borne out by the data. On the other hand, although the government aims to push for increased shareholder rights, as evident in recent presidential decrees[38], there is only very weak evidence that it uses its voting rights to cause management to honour shareholder rights.

With respect to 'L' the underlying specification seems to be quadratic, as the t-statistics of 'L^2' is larger than 2 and a Wald-test rejects the hypothesis that the coefficient of both variables should be 0 at the 5% level. The coefficient for 'L' is positive (and significant at the 10% level), but the coefficient

[38] For example, a presidential decree of July, 1, 1996 explicitly states the following: 'The capitalization of Russian companies should be increased in the following ways: Implementation of measures to increase the liquidity of the market, mainly by developing a system of protections for investor rights, including ... reducing the costs and risks of the system of securities circulation and servicing, and providing for greater information transparency of the market.'

Table 3.5. OLS Regressions with L

	OLS with robust standard errors	OLS with robust standard errors
Dependent variable	I_2 (Disclosure)	I_4 (Transfer)
Comm	214.913	387.784
	(0.908)	(1.030)
Electricity	202.915*	421.267**
	(1.919)	(2.064)
Metal	-72.755	-24.042
	(-1.326)	(-0.566)
Oil	-20.165	-34.790
	(-0.274)	(-0.395)
Trans	-86.292	-35.109
	(-1.328)	(-0.410)
e	0.004***	0.004
	(3.428)	(1.563)
L	5.900*	11.294**
	(1.839)	(2.449)
L^2	-0.153**	-0.232**
	(-2.569)	(-2.548)
State	2.962	5.304
	(1.434)	(1.599)
C	-3.911	-98.142
	(-0.050)	(-1.233)
N	140	140
R^2	0.3053	0.2596
adj. R^2	0.2573	0.2084
F-statistics	2.22	1.33
Prob (F-statistics)	0.0411	0.2269

t-values given in brackets. * denotes significance at the 10% level, ** at the 5% level and *** at the 1% level

of 'L^2' is negative and significant at the 5% level. The estimated coefficients imply that for outside stakes larger than 39%, shareholder friendliness starts to decrease. As 'L' is in general smaller than 39%, the basic effect of this variable is positive, but at a decreasing rate[39]. This would lend some credibility to

[39] Only in 13% of cases is the stake of the largest outside holder larger than 39%. The negative effect in the case of the very large outside holdings could be due to the fact that management, together with the largest outside blockholder, own so many shares that it is impossible to commit not to expropriate minority interests. This might be the case if together they own more than 75% and therefore can change the company charter at their discretion. They will not introduce

Table 3.6. PROBIT Regressions with L

	probit with robust std errors marginal effects	probit with robust std errors marginal effects	probit with robust std errors marginal effects
Dependent var.	I_1 (ADR)	I_3 (Indep)	I_5 (IAS)
Comm	0.196	0.034	0.106
	(1.479)	(0.256)	(0.659)
Electricity	0.046	0.327*	-0.113
	(0.456)	(1.924)	(-0.749)
Metal	-0.110	-0.126	-0.120
	(-1.543)	(-1.581)	(-1.153)
Oil	-0.033	0.112	0.136
	(-0.473)	(1.089)	(1.183)
Trans	0.059	-0.867	0.088
	(-0.530)	(-0.761)	(0.560)
e	8.98E-07*	1.37E-7	4.39E-6***
	(1.685)	(0.230)	(3.274)
L	-0.001	0.004	0.007
	(-0.167)	(0.677)	(1.096)
L^2	1.96E-5	-9.64E-5	-1.00E-4
	(0.279)	(-1.034)	(-0.997)
State	-0.002	0.002	0.002
	(-0.144)	(0.924)	(1.024)
N	140	140	140
Pseudo R^2	0.124	0.123	0.211
Prob¿chi^2	0.298	0.018	0.002

t-values given in brackets. * denotes significance at the 10% level, *** at the 1% level
For the dummy variables the marginal effect is for a discrete change from 0 to 1

proposition 3.2, i.e. that outside shareholders bargain with management. As their bargaining power increases, they tend to be more successful in pushing for shareholder rights. They are also less likely to collude with management, as they can benefit less from expropriation. The data does not suggest that management has unlimited control in the absence of shareholder rights and proposition 3.1 would seem to be rejected by the data, as for this case the model in section 3.2.1 would imply a negative sign for 'L'. The positive coef-

shareholder rights if there are some arbitrarily small costs associated with the introduction.

ficient would also make it harder to argue that '*L*' is endogenous. If it was, it would be expected that following *La Porta et al (1996)* concentrated shareholdings act as a substitute for shareholder rights. This does not seem to be the case.

With respect to the industry dummies, only 'Electricity' is significant (at the 10% level) and has a positive coefficient. The communications industry has the largest (and positive) coefficient of all industries, but is insignificant at the 10% level. 'Metal' has the smallest coefficient, but it is not significant at the 10% level. This is roughly in line with investment needs, as indicated by growth and price changes in the different industries. According to this measure, it is the communications industry which has the largest, and the metals industry which has the lowest investment needs. Therefore, there is some weak evidence that the industry dummies act as a proxy for returns from future investment, n [40]. With respect to I_4 the coefficients of the independent variables have the same sign and similar significance levels, but the overall regression is not significant.

With respect to the regressions for the binary indicators I_1, I_3 and I_5, it should first be noted that the I_1 regression is not significant at the 10% level. Consequently the focus should be on the other two regressions. With respect to the I_3- and the I_5-regressions, the signs of the coefficients are the same as they are for the continuous variables. However, fewer of them are significant at the 10% level. For the I_5-regression only the coefficient of 'e' is significant (at the 1% level) and for the I_3-regression it is only the coefficient of 'Electricity' which is significant (at the 10% level). The ordering of the coefficients for the industry dummies is roughly in line with the I_2 and I_4 regressions, but the oil industry has a relatively larger coefficient. Overall, it seems that the model outlined can explain more of the behaviour of firms with respect to information disclosure (I_2, I_5) than with respect to the independence of shareholder registries (I_4, I_3) or whether ADRs are outstanding. One hypothesis to explain this would be that improvements with respect to the protection of property rights of shareholder have led to a situation where the most obvious violations, like the obstruction of the transfer of ownership of shares by management, are not possible any more, even in case shareholder registries are not fully independent. Therefore, violations might now be more reflected in problems of the provision of information, which is why shareholders as well as firms might focus more on these issues.

The regressions of tables 3.5 and 3.6 have to be interpreted with care as it is not entirely clear whether '*L*' is truly exogenous. However, there is no obvious instrument available and it turns out that the sign of the coefficient is the opposite of what one would expect under the hypothesis of endogeneity. Nevertheless, the following table (3.7) reports the results when omitting '*L*'.

[40] It is noteworthy that the investment needs relevant for this analysis are the ones that are to be fulfilled by share-issues. In the case of oil-firms, for example, it could be the case that new projects are mainly implemented by joint ventures with foreign firms, which would raise a large part of the required finance.

Table 3.7. OLS Regressions without L

	OLS with robust standard errors	OLS with robust standard errors
Dependent variable	I_2 (Disclosure)	I_4 (Transfer)
Comm	190.824	392.494
	(0.822)	(1.073)
Electricity	103.478	329.884*
	(1.059)	(1.825)
Metal	-89.202	-46.221
	(-1.653)	(-1.177)
Oil	-62.790	-63.785
	(-0.802)	(-0.651)
Trans	-95.316	-42.835
	(-1.405)	(-0.487)
e	0.003***	0.003
	(3.318)	(1.483)
State	3.650*	5.366
	(1.675)	(1.517)
C	19.598	-13.029
	(0.744)	(-0.202)
N	140	140
R^2	0.2795	0.2357
adj. R^2	0.2413	0.1932
F-statistics	2.44	1.36
Prob (F-statistics)	0.0220	0.2277

t-values given in brackets. * denotes significance at the 10% level, *** at the 1% level

Overall, dropping the 'L' and 'L^2' does not affect the coefficients of the remaining variables. It is still the case that the coefficient of 'e' is positive and significant. The relative signs of the coefficients of the industry dummies are still roughly in line with the hypothesis on investment needs, but remain mostly insignificant. The only new result is that in the I_2 regression the variable 'State' is now significant at the 5% level, giving some limited evidence for an active state involvement with respect to the issue of shareholder rights. In the appendix, I provide regressions with 'L', but without 'L^2'. In most of the regressions, 'L' alone is insignificant. The appendix also reports the 3SLS estimate of the system of equations when PE is included in the 'shareholder rights' regressions. It is noteworthy, that PE is never significant and in some

Table 3.8. PROBIT Regressions without L

	probit, robust standard errors, marginal effects	probit, robust standard errors, marginal effects	probit, robust standard errors, marginal effects
Dependent variable	I_1 (ADR)	I_3 (Indep)	I_5 (IAS)
Comm	0.210	0.013	0.148
	(1.596)	(0.105)	(0.912)
Electricity	0.066	0.222*	-0.110
	(0.720)	(1.721)	(-0.806)
Metal	-0.109	-0.130	-0.127
	(-1.544)	(-1.619)	(-1.225)
Oil	-0.025	0.085	0.153
	(-0.431)	(0.913)	(1.374)
Trans	0.062	-0.088	0.087
	(0.559)	(-0.746)	(0.556)
e	9.17E-7*	1.30E-7	4.39E-6***
	(1.651)	(0.219)	(3.433)
State	-0.001	0.002	0.001
	(-0.331)	(1.334)	(0.678)
N	140	140	140
Pseudo R^2	0.124	0.115	0.204
Prob¿chi^2	0.298	0.026	0.001

t-values given in brackets. * denotes significance at the 10% level, *** at the 1% level
For the dummy variables the marginal effect is for a discrete change from 0 to 1

specifications has a negative sign (i.e. contrary to the theoretical prediction if it was to proxy for growth potential).

The following tables aim to provide a test of proposition 3.3, by estimating equation 3.13. In particular, it is tested whether increased shareholder friendliness is reflected in a higher valuation of the firm. The p/e ratio is for the end of January 1996. As has been argued above, the indicators for shareholder rights are endogenous and therefore have to be instrumented. Given the regressions in table 3.5 the obvious instruments are 'State', 'e' and 'L'. In the first set of regressions, only the index z_1 is used to capture shareholder friendliness to minimize problems of multicollinearity among the different measures of shareholder friendliness. Only using z_1 also means that there are a sufficient number of instruments. However, as pointed out above, the index is to some extent still arbitrary, in spite of the principal components analysis. Therefore, the second set of equations uses individual indicators.

As the number of instruments limits the number of indicators , two different equations are estimated: First, I_2, I_3 and I_5 are put into the regression, as the individual regressions explaining those three variables were the most significant ones. Second, the indicators I_1, I_2 and I_4 are put into the regression, as those were identified by the principal components analysis to be the three indicators which account for most of the variation in the five indicators. As discussed above, industry dummies are put in as a proxy for growth prospects. Lastly, an estimate for beta is included into the regression to control for the required return on capital. This beta has been estimated using weekly returns which were available for 32 shares between 29 November 1995 and 13 September 1996 under the assumption that beta has been constant over time. As the market portfolio the 'RTS' (Russian Trading System) index was used. Although there is no turnover data available, the pattern of price changes suggests that there could be a non-trading bias in the estimates for beta. However, there is not sufficient data to estimate the Scholes-Williams estimator for beta which would correct for this problem. *Scholes and Williams* (1977) have shown that the infrequent trading bias leads to the estimated beta to be higher than the true beta for the more illiquid stocks and to be lower for the more liquid stocks. While this problem might bias results, it is in the absence of volume data unclear how serious the problem is. Potentially the shareprice data represents another deficiency in my dataset. Furthermore, to the extent that foreigners are the marginal investors in the Russian equity market, it might be the case that the correlation with the Russian market portfolio is misleading. Therefore, I also run the regression using the standard deviation ('stddev') to proxy for risk as opposed to the beta.

As it turns out, none of the regressions or variables has any significance[41]. This implies that proposition 3.3 is rejected by the data. Estimating the system with 3SLS by introducing PE into the shareholder rights regressions, as reported in the appendix, results in a positive and significant coefficient of I_2 in both systems of equations with 'beta' as well as with 'stddev' to proxy for risk. However, in the system with 'beta' the variable I_2 has a negative and significant coefficient. As only the coefficient of 'stddev' has the expected negative sign (but is not significant), whereas the coefficient of 'beta' has a positive coefficient, the specification with 'stddev' seems more reliable and the negative coefficient of I_2 should probably not be over-interpreted. While some of the conflicting results are presumably due to the poor quality of the data and the rather small sample, it nevertheless poses the question whether assumption 3.6 can be justified. In this sense, the above regressions show a limitation of the static model, in that the hypothesis that a higher PE should be associated with a higher shareholder friendliness depends on implicit assumptions on future expropriation. Depending on the assumption of

[41] However, *Nash and Willer (1995)* use a different measure for the valuation of some firms in the oil-industry and find that the variable 'Transfer' helps to explain differences in valuation.

Table 3.9. PE Regressions

	IV with robust standard errors	IV with robust standard errors
Dependent variable	PE	PE
z_1	5.778	6.666
	(0.258)	(0.429)
Div	-26.954	-34.296
	(-0.038)	(-0.070)
Stddev	0.099	
	(0.214)	
Beta		50.149
		(1.254)
Comm	-0.932	-6.239
	(-0.013)	(-0.128)
Electricity	-8.129	12.923
	(-0.123)	(0.321)
Metal	2.073	-8.303
	(0.046)	(-0.304)
Oil	10.261	-9.066
	(0.177)	(-0.247)
Trans	130.564	130.876
	(1.327)	(1.457)
C	-1.105	-8.528
	(-0.021)	(-0.210)
N	32	32
R^2	0.3649	0.4031
adj. R^2	0.1439	0.1955
F-statistics	0.73	0.76
Prob (F-statistics)	0.6611	0.6386

t-values given in brackets.

how stealing develops over time one could also construct models, where the p/e ratio is negatively associated with the shareholder rights. If, for example, managers can only expropriate profits that have not been announced, stealing would be reflected in the announced p/e ratio. If, furthermore, some mechanism would stop expropriation in the future, the correlation between the p/e ratio and shareholder friendliness would be negative. Market prices would reflect that there will be a jump in announced profits at the time when expropriation will stop. In the next chapter a model is proposed where the timing of the end of stealing is endogenously derived. A more fundamental problem with the *PE* regressions has already been mentioned above:

Table 3.10. PE Regressions without Index

	IV with robust std errors	IV with robust std errors	IV with robust std errors	IV with robust std errors
Dep. Var.	PE	PE	PE	PE
Disclosure	0.269	-0.928	-0.144	-0.138
	(0.150)	(-0.072)	(-0.533)	(-0.577)
Transfer			0.080	0.074
			(0.610)	(0.664)
ADR			-57.056	-1.566
			(-0.419)	(-0.012)
Indep	798.815	-1514.313		
	(0.132)	(-0.075)		
IAS	-333.110	621.026		
	(-0.145)	(0.072)		
Div	-3373.646	12799.27	1072.399	806.019
	(-0.141)	(0.074)	(0.804)	(0.715)
Stddev		-12.588		-0.255
		(-0.074)		(-0.483)
Beta	7.785		67.541	
	(0.021)		(1.071)	
Comm	-613.683	1688.224	58.907	32.008
	(-0.134)	(0.075)	(0.644)	(0.395)
Electricity	-789.745	2295.474	39.870	11.106
	(-0.131)	(0.074)	(0.572)	(0.170)
Metal	-454.736	1346.702	-12.208	7.653
	(-0.136)	(0.075)	(-0.324)	(0.214)
Oil	-494.940	1523.574	25.852	43.435
	(-0.133)	(0.075)	(0.472)	(0.810)
Trans	-89.152	692.754	148.427	124.902
	(-0.051)	(0.093)	(1.288)	(1.232)
C	305.595	-872.882	-44.049	-23.805
	(0.136)	(-0.074)	(-0.731)	(-0.539)
N	32	32	32	32
R^2	0.0000	0.0000	0.1189	0.2269
adj. R^2	-	-	-0.3081	-0.1412
F-statistics	0.06	0.19	0.25	0.41
Prob (F-statistics)	1.000	0.9946	0.9370	0.9242

t-values given in brackets.

the earnings from the Russian accounts need not be correlated with earnings derived according to the international accounting principles.

There is some more direct evidence for assumption 3.6. Table 3.11 shows that the correlation of the number of share-issues a firm has undertaken and the indicators of behaviour towards shareholders are positively correlated. This implies that management indeed treats shareholders well in order to raise new capital.

Table 3.11. Correlation Between Issues and Shareholder Rights

License	0.202 (0.019)
Transfer	0.141 (0.105)
IAS	0.177 (0.040)
Disclose	0.277 (0.001)
ADR	0.294 (0.001)

p-values in brackets

However, it has to be borne in mind that in many of these share-issues no new capital has been raised. In general, most of the new shares were allocated to the shareholders when the capital of a firm was revalued; the firms did not receive any new capital. However, these re-valuations occurred equally frequently in all firms. Once a year the Ministry of Finance released instructions to change the charter capital and it is likely that most firms followed those instructions. Therefore, a higher than average number of issues is likely to reflect genuine share issues that did raise new capital. This effect is illustrated by table 3.11[42].

3.5 Conclusion

To the extent that privatisation resulted in strong de facto insider control, which is not necessarily reflected in formal ownership, there is likely to be a significant agency problem. While in principle the resulting problems can be mitigated by introducing laws on property rights (i.e. on shareholder as well as creditor rights), law enforcement is often difficult during the development

[42] One of the most publicized share issues had been carried out by the Red October Chocolate Factory in 1995.

of capital markets. In particular, management is likely to expropriate shareholders. This, in turn, is likely to lead to underinvestment. However, this chapter shows that a few firms seem to honour shareholder rights to some extent. This might partly be due to two different factors.

First, self interest might cause management to start to honour shareholder rights. If the potential returns to investment that accrue to management in its role as a shareholder outweigh the utility-loss from reduced control over the firm, management might be more willing to honour shareholder rights. The significance of employment, which I take as a proxy for the expected value of expropriation, would tend to support this hypothesis. Furthermore, weak evidence that investment needs as proxied by industry dummies matter also gives some evidence that this effect plays a role.

Second, outside pressures might be strong enough to force management to introduce shareholder rights. This chapter has presented some limited evidence that the largest outside investor has some bargaining power that can be used to introduce shareholder rights. However, this effect becomes weaker for very large shareholders (who might not necessarily choose to push for shareholder rights). Furthermore, there is some limited evidence that at the very least the state does not hinder the introduction of shareholder rights and might even be a (weak) positive force.

The study of how shareholder rights are related to forward looking measures of market valuation of firms shows that the static analysis of this chapter has to be complemented by an analysis of the dynamics and the changes in ownership in particular. This is examined theoretically in the following chapter.

3.6 Appendix

3.6.1 The Index z_1

Algebraically, the principal components analysis aims to find the linear combination of the set of variables that provides the best fit to all individual variables. This is done by a regression of the linear combination

$$z_1 = Ic_1 \tag{3.14}$$

on I, where c_1 is a vector that contains the weights for the individual indices I_1 to I_5. Since the regressions of any column of I on z_1 will be equivalent for any scalar multiple of c_1 the indeterminacy can be removed by imposing

$$z_1' z_1 = 1. \tag{3.15}$$

Minimizing the residuals of the regression results in a vector c_1^* and with

$$z_1^* = Ic_1^* \tag{3.16}$$

gives the index z_1^*. Applying this method to the five indicators I_1 to I_5, standardized to mean 0 and standard deviation of 1, leads to the following principal component:

$$z_1^* = I \begin{bmatrix} 0.119 \\ 0.491 \\ 0.074 \\ 0.347 \\ 0.082 \end{bmatrix} \tag{3.17}$$

The first principal component accounts for 90% of the variation in the five variables.

3.6.2 Additional Data and Regressions

Table 3.12. List of Variables

ADR	Dummy for outstanding issue of ADR, GDR or RDC, as of 08/1996
beta	covariance of returns of share with RTS index over variance of RTS index for 11/1995 to 9/1996
Comm	Dummy for communications industry
Disclosure	Survey measure for openness with respect to information, Q1 1996
Div	Dividend pay-out ratio for fiscal year 1994, announced 1995
e	Employment, as of 01/1996
Electricity	Dummy for electricity industry
IAS	Dummy for hiring international accountancy firm for fiscal year 1995
L	Amount of shares of largest outside blockholder, as of 01/1996
License	Dummy for use of licensed share registry, as of 08/1996
Metal	Dummy for metal industry
Oil	Dummy for oil and gaz and chemical industry
PE	price earnings ratio as of 01/1996
Stddev	standard deviation of returns of share for 11/1995 to 9/1996
Transport	Dummy for transportation industry
Transfer	Survey measure concerning ease of transfer of ownership, Q1 1996
State	Amount of shares held by the state, as of 01/1996
z−1	index of shareholder rights weighted average of Disclosure, Transfer, ADR, IAS, License

Table 3.13. Shareholder Rights by Industry

	Comm	Electricity	Metal	Oil & gas	Transport	Other	Sum
% in industry with	6.4	9.3	29.3	23.6	8.5	22.9	100.0
ADR	33.3	23.1	2.4	12.1	8.3	6.4	10.0
IAS	33.3	15.4	9.8	45.5	25.0	21.8	24.3
License (LR)	22.2	38.5	4.9	27.3	8.3	15.3	17.1
ADR & IAS	33.3	15.4	0.0	12.1	0.0	2.9	7.1
ADR & LR	22.2	23.1	0.0	6.1	0.0	0.0	5.0
IAS & LR	22.2	15.4	0.0	15.2	8.3	2.9	7.8
ADR & IAS & LR	22.2	15.4	0.0	6.1	0.0	0.0	4.3

Table 3.14. Ownership by Industry

	Comm	Electricity	Metal	Oil & gas	Transport	Other	Sum
Mean no. of outside blocks	1.6	1.5	1.6	1.5	1.5	2.2	1.7
Mean holding:							
Outside blocks	31.8	48.4	26.3	31.2	19.3	28.1	29.7
Largest block	27.7	44.3	18.1	27.7	12.7	18.3	23.0
Holding/FIG	22.1	43.6	1.0	20.6	0.0	3.4	11.4
Non-fin. firm	2.2	2.1	10.5	1.7	6.6	10.2	6.7
Investment fund	0.8	0.0	4.6	1.2	4.5	6.3	3.5
Bank	0.6	0.0	5.7	4.4	2.4	2.4	3.5
Frgn. fin. firm	4.5	1.7	2.0	2.2	3.1	1.2	2.1
State	25.0	5.5	8.9	16.9	25.7	9.2	13.0

Table 3.15. Measures of Association*

	Independent	Variables			
	ADR	Indep	IAS	Disclosure	Transfer
Dependent Variables					
ADR	-	3.263	3.777	3.487	3.010
Indep	3.263	-	2.680	2.653	2.567
IAS	3.777	2.680	-	2.563	2.422

*: t-statistic of logit regressions of dependent variable on one independent variable including constant

Table 3.16. OLS Regressions without L^2

	OLS with robust standard errors	OLS with robust standard errors
Dependent variable	I_4 (Transfer)	I_2 (Disclosure)
Comm	404.958	226.286
	(1.077)	(0.957)
Electricity	347.714*	154.207
	(1.803)	(1.507)
Metal	-45.415	-86.909
	(-1.170)	(-1.635)
Oil	-53.053	-32.259
	(-0.575)	(-0.438)
Trans	-41.045	-90.223
	(-0.471)	(-1.384)
E	0.003	0.003***
	(1.474)	(3.226)
L	-0.723	-2.058*
	(-0.451)	(-1.661)
State	5.070	2.807
	(1.541)	(1.380)
C	-2.021	62.418
	(0.036)	(0.930)
N	140	140
R^2	0.2362	0.2865
F-statistics	1.29	2.12
Prob (F-statistics)	0.2545	0.0382

t-values given in brackets. * denotes significance at the 10% level, *** at the 1% level

Table 3.17. PROBIT Regressions without L^2

	probit, robust standard errors, marginal effects	probit, robust standard errors, marginal effects	probit, robust standard errors, marginal effects
Dep. var.	I_1 (ADR)	I_3 (Indep)	I_5 (IAS)
Comm	0.192	0.039	0.111
	(1.452)	(0.290)	(0.683)
Electricity	0.050	0.272*	-0.136
	(0.504)	(1.829)	(-0.947)
Metal	-0.109	-0.128	-0.128
	(-1.531)	(-1.596)	(-1.227)
Oil	-0.032	0.107	0.127
	(-0.468)	(1.054)	(1.095)
Trans	0.060	-0.086	0.083
	(0.544)	(-0.726)	(0.527)
E	5.54E-6*	9.23E-7	4.32E-6***
	(1.696)	(0.165)	(3.356)
L	0.003	-0.001	0.002
	(0.312)	(-0.622)	(0.754)
State	-0.001	1.89E-4	0.002
	(-0.132)	(0.937)	(0.977)
N	140	140	140
Pseudo R^2	0.124	0.117	0.201
Prob¿chi^2	0.225	0.042	0.001

t-values given in brackets. * denotes significance at the 10% level, *** at the 1% level

For the dummy variables the marginal effect is for a discrete change from 0 to 1

Table 3.18. Three Stage Least Squares Regressions without Index

	3SLS			3SLS		
Dep. Var.	PE	Discl.	Transfer	PE	Discl.	Transfer
Comm	5.35	-150.49	-230.93	-34.77	79.37	466.68
	(0.073)	(-0.319)	(-0.326)	(-0.466)	(0.140)	(0.826)
Elec-tricity	-20.01	110.50	423.59	-56.19	79.87	502.93
	(-0.327)	(0.331)	(0.845)	(-0.972)	(0.191)	(1.180)
Metal	-20.71	-433.25	-294.70	-93.12	-420.74	-110.46
	(-0.402)	(-1.377)	(-0.617)	(-1.555)	(-1.042)	(-0.276)
Oil	24.70	-5.28	-286.47	-16.00	156.26	430.80
	(0.420)	(-0.012)	(-0.443)	(-0.280)	(0.359)	(0.991)
Trans	104.44**	-226.63	-2472.04	55.19	603.71	805.00
	(2.208)	(-0.164)	(-1.209)	(0.999)	(0.541)	(0.694)
E		0.01*	0.00		0.01***	0.01***
		(1.855)	(1.085)		(2.903)	(3.679)
L		-4.34	60.11		-28.50	-26.87
		(-0.077)	(0.696)		(-0.651)	(-0.559)
L^2		-0.06	-1.12		0.41	0.42
		(-0.057)	(-0.706)		(0.526)	(0.474)
State		6.90	14.55*		3.05	7.02
		(1.289)	(1.932)		(0.501)	(1.069)
C	-4.94	299.92	-449.28	17.77	381.51	-50.29
	(-0.104)	(0.801)	(-0.784)	(0.350)	(0.983)	(-0.127)
PE		-0.92	15.99		-5.66	-4.80
		(-0.108)	(1.274)		(0.983)	(0.693)
Div	802.07			1305.92		
	(0.860)			(1.498)		
Stddev	-0.14					
	(-0.254)					
Beta				48.95		
				(1.037)		
Discl.	-0.20			-0.43***		
	(-1.382)			(-2.621)		
Transf.	0.12*			0.26***		
	(1.690)			(2.861)		
N	32	32	32	32	32	32
R^2	0.069	0.494	-0.680	-1.087	0.094	0.435
chi^2	22.65	35.65	32.15	29.67	20.49	41.29
Prob (chi^2)	0.007	0.000	0.000	0.005	0.025	0.000

t-values given in brackets. * denotes significance at the 10% level, ** at the 5% level and *** at the 1% level

4. Corporate Governance without State Guaranteed Shareholder Rights

4.1 Introduction

In the previous chapter a simple model has been proposed to provide a framework to analyse the behaviour of management with respect to outside shareholders. The main limitation of that model is that it is embedded in a static setting and does not allow for changes in ownership. However, as reported in chapter 1, ***Blasi and Shleifer (1996)*** and ***Blasi et al (1997)*** find that the ownership of top management is increasing over time. This chapter addresses these dynamic aspects by developing a richer model where management can acquire or sell shares in the firm. The chapter argues that the problem of the lack of shareholder rights should be mitigated, but most likely only in the long run. In particular, this chapter analyses a game between managers and investors, where managers have the choice to introduce shareholder rights or not. The introduction of shareholder rights limits the amount of profits that can be stolen[1]. Investors are only willing to finance new projects if they anticipate earning the required rate of return. In such a set-up managers realize that they can be better off honouring shareholder rights as the amount of new projects they can undertake can be very limited without the guarantee of such rights. Furthermore, if managers want to sell some of their own shares they are interested in high shareprices and therefore in honouring shareholder rights. However, this chapter shows that in the short run, these effects are only strong enough if management already owns a large enough percentage of shares at the outset. This is true since introducing shareholder rights also carries a cost. In particular, outsiders might gain control once shareholder rights have been introduced and consequently management might lose its private benefits from running the firm. If it wants to remain in control, management has in general to buy up further shares. The introduction of share-

[1] Evidence for stealing by management is, for example, provided by the surveys of the 'New Russia Barometer' *(Rose, 1995)*. When employees were asked whether management would take money or assets from the enterprise for their private benefit, 16% of the respondents answered 'to a great extent' and another 30% 'to some extent' (excluding the 'Don't knows' from the sample).

holder rights increases the price of the shares management wants to acquire. Secondly, a commitment to shareholder rights decreases the opportunities to divert profits for management's personal consumption. The smaller the fraction of profits management owns formally, the more valuable is the possibility to divert profits. As a result, these costs outweigh the benefits if management owns an insufficient amount of shares at the outset. Only if management owns enough shares as a result of the privatisation procedures, the problem of weak enforcement mechanisms of state-guaranteed shareholder rights is mitigated in the short run. Alternatively, if it is very difficult for management to 'launder' the profits they have diverted and to re-deploy them inside their firm, shareholder rights also might be introduced.

In the long run, more firms start to honour shareholder rights, even if management did not receive any shares in the privatisation process and if money laundering is possible. This is true, as management can steal profits for some time and use these stolen profits to build up a stake in the firm sufficiently large to signal to investors that shareholder rights will be introduced in the subsequent period. The share ownership of management then serves as a commitment device for the introduction of shareholder rights in the future. However, the fewer shares management received, the longer it can take until shareholder rights are introduced.

The chapter is to be seen in the context of the literature on management behaviour in transition economies. The focus of the existing literature has been on how the behaviour of management is effected by privatisation, or the threat thereof (e.g. *Aghion et al (1994)*, or *Kocerba(1996)*). In particular, the *Aghion et al* model derives a policy conclusion similar to my model: managers should obtain shares in order to make them more willing to restructure. However, this chapter is not directly concerned with questions of what management does to the operation of the firm, but what it does to its ownership structure[2]. In this sense, the chapter is more closely related to parts of the finance literature. By focusing only on equity, it does not attempt to explain the capital structure of firms in transition economies. *Gomes (1996)* addresses similar issues (i.e. managements' choice of how many benefits to extract). He uses an asymmetric information setting where the true type of management is revealed over time by the observed level of extracted benefits. This makes the model very different from my model which is based on a moral hazard setting. Furthermore, his setting is one of an IPO decision, where management aims to sell shares. In my model, management does in general want to acquire more shares to consolidate control. Also, his paper is primarily concerned with private benefits (which are presumably very important, since it would otherwise be possible in many more cases to bribe incompetent management out of their jobs), whereas this chapter mainly focuses on financial (and contractible) benefits. This seems fair in the con-

[2] However, in this model management chooses the size of the capital stock.

text of transition economies, where a large part of profits tends to disappear unrecorded (see *Nash and Willer, 1995*).

In spite of all these differences, the serious question must be posed whether an asymmetric information setting or a moral hazard setting is more appropriate as a model strategy. I believe that the moral hazard approach is appropriate for several reasons. First, on a very general level, the transition to market economies is largely one of changing incentives and changing behaviour in response to new incentives. Second, in the environment of transition economies, where information is very scarce as well as highly noisy, it is, *ceteris paribus*, more difficult to signal types of management to potential investors than in OECD type economies. In particular, the level of private benefit expropriation is unlikely to be observed. Third, models that are based on reputation building run into the problem that in the last period of a game there is no gain from keeping up a reputation. As transition in general means progressing from one state to another, it is natural to think of transition of a process that has a last period. Once firms have reached the state where they have caught up with their capital expenditure program, they would tend to expropriate investors. Similar to the models of external borrowing (for example *Eaton, Gersovitz and Stiglitz*, 1986), this would be anticipated by investors and Russian firms would in general not receive any capital. In this context it seems more appropriate to think about a bonding device as opposed to reputation building. Nevertheless, similar results might well be obtained in an asymmetric information setting. There could well be good and bad managers, i.e. 'stealing' and 'honest' ones. Honest managers have an exogenously given utility function where they derive negative utility from stealing. The signal managers can send might be to refrain from diluting shareholders, as dilution seems more easily observable than stealing of profits. Depending on the associated costs and benefits, there might well be separating as well as pooling equilibria. In the pooling equilibrium, both stealing and honest managers do not dilute and get access to capital, but only slowly over time as their reputation for honesty grows. In a separating equilibrium costs and benefits are such that stealing management would choose to dilute, whereas honest management would not dilute. This would increase the speed with which honest managers would get access to capital. At the same time it would mean that stealing management would not get any capital at all. In such a model, the problem that management wants to remain in control would also slow down the maximum speed of the accumulation of capital, just as in my model. As long as the assumption is made that management wants to remain in control, the social optimum is in general not reached even if other modelling techniques are employed, at least if the funding possibilities are restricted to equity issues. The main difference between a reputation building model outlined above and my model would be that there would be even more heterogeneity between different firms, whereas in my model the difference is likely to disappear over time. However, to assume exogenously that there are managers with a disutility from stealing and others without such disutility is a strong assumption.

On a more general level, the chapter addresses the issue of corporate control. *Hart and Moore (1990)* and *Aghion and Bolton (1992)* are the classic papers in this domain. These papers address the question how to get borrowers to transfer non-verifiable revenues to the lender. In my case, revenues are known, but the legal system is insufficient to force firms to make such transfers. A more important difference is that *Hart* and *Moore* as well as *Aghion* and *Bolton* focus mostly on debt, whereas this chapter analyses equity in its role of allocating control rights. In this sense, the chapter is more closely related to *Grossman and Hart (1980)* who analyse the take-over mechanism and its efficiency in allocating control over the firms. In my model there are no differences in ability between different managers or owners and therefore, allocative efficiency is not of prime importance. Instead, this chapter analyses constraints of investment due to the desire of management to keep in control. For illustrative purposes this chapter refers to the case of Russia, but it is to be seen in the wider context of transition economies.

In the following section, the basic set-up of a two-period model is described. In particular, the decision problem for both players, management and investors, is laid out, followed by a description of the precise timing and the equilibrium concept. The analysis of the two-period model starts with a characterization of the optimal dividend policy, which is the starting point for the analysis of whether shareholder rights are introduced. Overall, in the two-period case, three cases need to be considered. First, Section 4.2.6 describes the 'excess profitability case', where shareholder rights are never introduced. After deriving the capital stocks with and without shareholder rights, Section 4.2.7 describes two cases where shareholder rights are introduced: the cases of 'managerial entrenchment' and 'money-laundering'. The third part extends the model to three periods. Section 4.3.1 slightly changes the assumptions of the model in such a way that shareholder rights are *not* going to be introduced for the same reasons they were introduced in the two-period model. This allows to focus exclusively on an additional reason for their introduction which becomes relevant when a third period is added to the model. This new case, the 'commitment case' is described in section 4.3.2. The chapter concludes summarizing the model and derives hypotheses for empirical testing[3].

4.2 The Two Period Model

In the game to be analysed, there are two players: management and investors. The following section outlines their decision problems, followed by the timing of the game and the equilibrium concept employed.

[3] A list of the variables is in appendix A. All proofs are delegated to appendix B.

4.2.1 Management

The firms in an economy are at present controlled by their incumbent management, irrespective of the formal ownership structure. Shareholder rights have initially not been introduced. The introduction of shareholder rights is parameterised as a choice over the percentage of profits management can steal, φ_t. It can take on two values: $\bar{\varphi}_t$, given by the technology in the particular industry in the absence of shareholder rights, and $\underline{\varphi}_t$ $(< \bar{\varphi}_t)$ if management introduces shareholder rights, for example, by passing a company charter that guarantees such rights. Once shareholder rights have been introduced, φ_t is assumed to remain at the level $\underline{\varphi}_t$ for all subsequent periods. In this sense a corporate charter serves as a commitment device as in *Grossman and Hart (1980)*, such that management can credibly commit to stop diverting profits[4]. For algebraic convenience I set $\underline{\varphi}_t = 0$.

Management maximizes its utility of the following form

$$\max U(C_0, P_0) + \beta U(C_1, P_1) \tag{4.1}$$

where C_t denotes the consumption of a single good at time t, β is a discount factor and P_t are private (non-contractible) benefits the manager obtains from being in control of the firm, for $t \in [0, 1]$. For simplicity I

[4] For example, many Russian firms have a clause in their charter which states that the maximum amount of votes an individual investor can exert at a shareholder meeting is 1% of total votes - even if this investor owns a much higher percentage of the outstanding shares. Once this clause is removed from the charter, it would seem difficult to re-introduce it as this requires a 75% majority.

Also, disclosing information can help to commit to steal less. If, for example, the size of oil reserves and the production capabilities are disclosed (employing an independent auditor) this information is unlikely to alter very quickly. This can make it harder for management to steal profits from oil production.

Other potential commitment devices include issuing American Depository Receipts (ADRs) which tend to increase the costs of the violation of shareholder rights. This is true as such a violation would get much more publicity and as a result increases the likelihood of state intervention (see chapter 3 for a more detailed discussion).

While the assumption of complete irreversibility is somewhat strong, it does seem to be the case that management can make a reversal more expensive. Whether these costs are sufficiently high to prevent reversals fully is an empirical question.

assume a linear utility function in order to be able to abstract from the issue of consumption smoothing. This seems appropriate since consumption smoothing does not seem to be the driving force behind the development of corporate governance in transition economies[5]. Furthermore, I set the rate of time preference $\beta = \frac{1}{1+r}$, where r is the risk-free interest rate.

If management is in control, private benefits amount to $\bar{P}$, otherwise they are 0. There are two ways to achieve this control. Either management does *not* introduce shareholder rights (and then is in control by default), or it does introduce shareholder rights but then must own more than θ percent of the total shares outstanding in order to obtain $\bar{P}$. Private benefits can thus be summarized in the following form:

$$P_t = \begin{cases} \bar{P} \; if \; \frac{\alpha_t}{\tau_t} \geq \theta \;\; or \;\; \varphi_t = \bar{\varphi}_t \\ 0 \;\; otherwise \end{cases}, \forall t \in [0, 1]. \tag{4.2}$$

Here α_t represents the number of shares management owns in period t and τ_t denotes the total amount of shares outstanding in the same period. Private benefits $\bar{P}$ are assumed to be so large, that management is under no circumstances willing to lose control of the firm. Some evidence for this assumption is given by *Blasi et al (1997)*. They report that in 1994 outsiders were in general denied directors on the board, although they owned on average 21% of the firm in their sample. Only in a few cases did outsiders and insiders find a compromise which resulted in some outside representation on the boards. This left the large majority of firms in the control of management. From 1995 the representation of outsiders rose. This was mainly achieved not through open voting in shareholder meetings, but through private deals between management and some outsiders. In 1996 31% of seats were held by outsiders. However, this figure is likely to overstate the true extent of outside influence, as firms controlled by management might be included among investors labelled as outside investors. Also, it is likely, that outsiders gain representation more easily in firms which are less valuable (where more restructuring is necessary), as insiders fight less in order to keep these assets under their control. In any case, even a board representation of 31% is not enough to exert control against the 69% held by management and the state, in particular, as the state until 1996 in general voted in line with managements' proposals. This would still leave the majority of Russia's valuable firms in the control of management. Similarly, *Blasi et al (1997)* report that of the 30% of firms that had exchanged their directors between 1992 and 1996, 80% of the replacements were from within the company. Furthermore, as late as in 1996, 60% of managers were opposed to making financial data available to

[5] The results and mechanisms are robust when a standard logarithmic utility function is used.

outside investors[6]. *Boycko et al (1995)* also report that some managers physically threaten challengers at shareholder meetings, rig shareholder votes or illegally change corporate charters. All these pieces of evidence show how management aims to stay in control of the firms. Therefore, $\frac{\alpha_i}{\tau_i} \geq \theta$ becomes an additional restriction in case management introduces shareholder rights.

The firm under management's control is the only source of management's income and management has zero wealth at the outset of the game. Management's budget constraint therefore depends on the profit of the firm $\pi(\cdot)$, which is increasing in last period's capital stock , K_{t-1}.

$$[\varphi_t + \frac{\alpha_{t-1}}{\tau_{t-1}}(1-\varphi_t)\gamma_t]\pi(K_{t-1}) = (\alpha_t - \alpha_{t-1})p_t + C_t, \forall t \in [0,1] \qquad (4.3)$$

where γ_t is the percentage of the remaining profit (after management diverted the fraction φ_t) that is paid out as dividends to shareholders. The income of management consists therefore of the percentage of profit it diverts (φ_t), as well as its share ($\frac{\alpha_{t-1}}{\tau_{t-1}}$) of the remaining profit, which is paid out as dividends. This income is used either for consumption or for purchases of further shares by management. Shares trade at the price p_t. Management can also sell shares to boost its income in a given period. It is assumed that it is not possible for management or the firm to borrow money (or to sell the stock short). The fact that the majority of firms in transition economies are in fact not able to obtain credit apart from very short-term working capital credits justifies this assumption[7]. The profit function takes the form

$$\pi(K_{t-1}) = \{ \begin{matrix} (1+a)K_{t-1} & if\ K_{t-1} \leq K^* \\ 0 & if\ K_{t-1} > K^* \end{matrix}, \forall t \in [0,1] \qquad (4.4)$$

[6] A good example of how management cannot easily be made accountable to outside shareholders is the case of Komineft, where management in 1994 diluted outside shareholders in an apparently illegal manner. This violation could not be rectified by a court as laws were unclear and the local administration on the side of management.

[7] Interestingly, one of the few significant lenders in many transition economies, the EBRD, does not lend to firms that violate shareholder rights (See *EBRD, 1997*). If such behaviour of potential lenders was widespread, the incentives to introduce shareholder rights might be even stronger than in a model without debt.

Lending is also not explicitly modelled. While in reality managers are able to lend, this restriction is of no importance since I assume that the firms' projects are so profitable at the given level of investment that management would never choose to lend at rate r.

where a, the marginal product of capital, is larger than the interest rate r. Profits are modelled as gross profits and are always larger than K_{t-1} because depreciation is for simplicity set to 100%.

The capital stock at the end of period t, K_t, depends on management's choice of how much of this period's profits to divert and how much to pay out in the form of dividends. The remaining profit is complemented by proceeds from a share issue, such that K_t is of the following form:

$$K_t = (1-\gamma_t)(1-\varphi_t)\pi(K_{t-1}) + s_t p_t \tag{4.5}$$

where s_t is the number of new shares issued by management in period t at price p_t. A strategy S_m for management comprises for every period t the set $\{\varphi_{t+1}, \alpha_t, s_t, \gamma_t\}$. The parameters s_0 and φ_2 are irrelevant since the game finishes after period 1. Figure 4.1 provides an overview over management's actions and shareholdings as well as over the development of the capital stock:

Period 0		Period 1		
t_{-1}		t_0		t_1
State Variables	**Decisions**	**State Variables**	**Decisions**	
$\frac{\alpha_{-1}}{\tau_{-1}}$	α_0	$\frac{\alpha_0}{\tau_{-1}+s_0}$	α_1	
	C_0		C_1	
K_{-1}	γ_0	K_0	γ_1	
	ϕ_1			
	s_0			

Fig. 4.1. The Game Managers Play

4.2.2 Investors

In my model, there is an infinite amount of investors who act competitively. They have access not only to purchasing shares in firms but also to a risk-free asset which pays the rate r. Given that there is no uncertainty in the model, investors face no risk and require at least the return r if they are to acquire shares. When in period 0 investors compute the maximum price p_0 that would guarantee a return r, they have to take into account the amount of profits that are going to be stolen by management, as well as how many new shares are going to be issued. Investors can infer management's actions at any given future period. The maximum price investors would be prepared to pay in period 0 is

$$p_0 = \frac{\gamma_1(1-\varphi_1)\pi(K_0)}{\tau_0(1+r)} \tag{4.6}$$

The shareprice in period 0 equals the dividends paid out of post-stealing profits in the following (and last) period 1, discounted with the required rate of return r and divided by the amount of shares outstanding at the end of period 1, τ_0. This is the ex-dividend price, i.e. the price after γ_0% of non-stolen profits have been paid out in period 0. The underlying assumption is that the new shareholders acquire shares after dividends have been paid in period 0. In such a set-up the price in period 1 is 0, because the game ends before any dividends can be paid. A strategy S_i for investors comprises for every period t the maximum price they are willing to pay, given by the sequence $\{p_t\}$.

4.2.3 Timing

In both periods management first determines whether to introduce shareholder rights or not. Consumption in period t equals management's residual income. At the same time, management decides how many new shares to issue. Having learned whether shareholder rights are introduced or not as well as how many shares are being issued and how large the capital stock will be, investors determine the maximum price at which they are willing to buy or sell shares. The total number of outstanding shares in the next period is the sum of the new shares and the existing ones:

$$\tau_t = \tau_{-1} + s_0 \tag{4.7}$$

4.2.4 Equilibrium Concept

DEFINITION 4.1: An equilibrium is a pair of strategies (S_m, S_i), such that
(i) S_m is a solution to the following problem

$$\max_{C_t, K_t, \alpha_t, s_t, \varphi_t} U(C_0, P_0) + \frac{1}{1+r}U(C_1, P_1), s.t.$$

$$[\varphi_t + \frac{\alpha_{t-1}}{\tau_{t-1}}(1-\varphi_t)\gamma_t]\pi(K_{t-1}) = (\alpha_t - \alpha_{t-1})p_t + C_t$$

$$K_t = (1-\varphi_t)(1-\gamma_t)\pi(K_{t-1}) + s_t p_t$$

$$\tau_t = \tau_{-1} + s_0$$

$$P_t = \begin{cases} \bar{P} \; if \; \frac{\alpha_t}{\tau_t} \geq \theta \; \; or \; \varphi_t = \bar{\varphi}_t \\ 0 \; otherwise \end{cases}$$

$$C_t \geq 0, K_t \geq 0, s_t \geq -\tau_{-1}, 0 \leq \alpha_t, 0 \leq \gamma_t \leq 1, \varphi_t \in (\underset{-t}{\varphi}, \bar{\varphi}_t)$$

$\forall t \in \{0,1\}$, given initial conditions K_{-1},α_{-1} and τ_{-1}.
(ii) S_i consists of the following prices

$$S_i = \{p_0 = \frac{\gamma_1(1-\varphi_1)\pi(K_0)}{\tau_0(1+r)}, p_1 = 0\}$$

Condition (i) states that, given the prices set by investors, management maximizes its utility by choosing an optimal consumption stream as well as whether to stay in control of the firm. Condition (ii) requires that investors optimise in the following way: given that at least two homogeneous investors compete in a Bertrand fashion, they know that they will only obtain the shares if they bid at least the discounted expected value of the firm. Since investors can work out what actions management is going to implement they can use backward induction to determine the present value of the shares. They would never bid any more than that expected value since they would incur a loss.

The basic aim of this chapter is to analyse when management would choose to introduce shareholder rights, i.e. when to set $\varphi_1 = 0$. The basic trade-off is the following: Management can under some conditions increase the capital stock to higher levels by introducing shareholder rights. On the other hand, introducing shareholder rights means that less funds can be stolen (and consumed) in period 1. This would tend to make the introduction of shareholder rights more costly for management.

4.2.5 Optimal Dividends

This section serves to state the results concerning the dividend policy up front in order to facilitate the subsequent analysis.

LEMMA 4.1: It is optimal for management to pay out dividends worth 100% of profits in period 1 and it is never sub-optimal to not pay any dividends in period 0 if K^* is sufficiently large.

The intuition for the first part of the lemma is trivial. Given that the game finishes in period 1, it is optimal to consume all profits. Therefore, these profits must be paid out as dividends. The second half of the lemma needs a little explanation. If shareholder rights are introduced, it does not matter which pay-out ratio is chosen by management. In case more dividends are paid out, more new shares need to be issued. This means that management needs to buy up more new shares to remain in control. However, management also receives the dividends and therefore can afford to buy up the additional shares. As a result, the pay-out ratio does not matter. However, if shareholder rights are not going to be introduced, it is always optimal not to pay out any dividends. This is true because management profits more the larger the capital stock. And given that the capital stock in the absence of shareholder rights is constrained, management would never pay out any dividends. After all, such pay-outs would not only reduce the capital stock by the amount of the actual dividends, but would also leave less capital to back the new shares to be issued. For algebraic simplicity γ_1 will be set to 1 and γ_0 to 0 for the rest of the chapter, although in the case of the introduction of shareholder rights there are also equilibria where γ_0 is positive (associated with a larger share-issue s_0).

The result that firms which do not introduce shareholder rights do not pay out dividends is one testable implication of the model. The intuition is that management in firms without shareholder rights will always have an incentive to dilute existing shareholders. In this environment, any dividend would be like a gift to outside shareholders, which is not in the interest of management. However, the timing of dividend payments derived above is only due to the finite horizon of the game, and is not robust to increasing the number of periods of the model.

4.2.6 A Case where Shareholder Rights are Never Introduced

This section presents the 'excess profitability' case, in which shareholder rights will never be introduced. The rest of this chapter will abstract from this case.

PROPOSITION 4.1: In case $(1-\bar{\varphi}_1)(1+a) > (1+r)$ management never introduces shareholder rights.

In case $(1-\bar{\varphi}_1)(1+a) > (1+r)$, the post-stealing return of the investment is large enough to cover the required rate of return for the new investors. Therefore, management can raise any required capital stock even in the absence of shareholder rights. Given that the only benefit of shareholder rights is that a higher capital stock might be reached if they are introduced, management never has an incentive to introduce such rights in this case. Clearly, the more interesting case is the one where $(1-\bar{\varphi}_1)(1+a) < (1+r)$. From now on, this chapter assumes that this condition holds, requiring that post-stealing returns of the new project are too small to yield the required rate of return for new investors.

4.2.7 Two Cases where Shareholder Rights are Introduced

The benefit of introducing shareholder rights is a potentially higher capital stock, which results in higher profits. However, there are also costs of introducing shareholder rights. As a result, it is a necessary and not a sufficient condition for the capital stock to be higher with than without shareholder rights. In order to facilitate a clear presentation, this section first derives the necessary condition for the introduction of shareholder rights by calculating the capital stocks with and without shareholder rights. Only afterwards the sufficient condition for the introduction of shareholder rights is derived.

It is important to notice that even if new capital does not provide sufficient returns to investors in the absence of shareholder rights, management is nevertheless able to raise some finance without introducing shareholder rights:

LEMMA 4.2 (Dilution): If management finds it in its interest not to introduce shareholder rights and if the maximum capital stock, K^*, is sufficiently large, management always dilutes the present owners of the firm (including themselves) perfectly by issuing an infinite amount of shares, i.e. setting $s_0 -> \infty$.

The intuition is the following: If $(1-\bar{\varphi}_1)(1+a) < (1+r)$, the post-stealing returns of investment are not sufficient to pay for the required rate of return. Nevertheless, the firm can raise some finance if it has some old assets in place. The part of the old assets (and their returns) that cannot be stolen can assure to new investors that they will receive the required rate of return r. This works in the following way: The part of the new capital (and its profits) that cannot be stolen increases the value of the firm. By itself this increase would not be enough to pay for the cost of capital. Therefore, the share-price must fall, such that the new shareholders obtain the required return r. Such a fall decreases the wealth of the old shareholders. Issuing new shares is therefore like a wealth transfer to new shareholders. The wealth of the old shareholders is reduced and this reduction in wealth is used to compensate the new shareholders for the difference between the return on the new investment, $(1-\bar{\varphi}_1)(1+a)$, and the required return $(1+r)$. Since new shareholders always obtain the required return r, which is smaller than the return on the new capital, a, management must always gain from raising new capital (provided it is still smaller than K^*). The maximum capital stock is reached if the total wealth of the old shareholders is transferred to the new shareholders. This can be achieved by issuing an infinite amount of shares, perfectly diluting the old shareholders. It is noteworthy that dilution takes place, although shares are issued at the market price. However, this is the market price conditional on the fact that part of the new capital is going to be stolen. Therefore, this is similar to a situation where shares are sold below their market price. In appendix B it is shown that this results in the capital stock

$$K_0^{NR} = \frac{(1-\bar{\varphi}_0)\Pi(K_{-1})(1+r)}{1+r-(1-\bar{\varphi}_1)(1+a)} \tag{4.8}$$

The interpretation of K_0^{NR} is straightforward: management steals $\bar{\varphi}_0$ in period 0 and its remaining income is $(1-\bar{\varphi}_0)\Pi(K_{-1})$, since it dilutes the other owners perfectly. Multiplying this by $(1+r)$ translates period 0 into period 1 income. Of this income it must pledge $(1+r)-(1-\bar{\varphi}_1)(1+a)$

for every unit of new capital it attracts, which it does by giving 100% of ownership to the new investors. This results in capital stock K_0^{NR}.

In the next step this capital stock is compared with the one in the absence of shareholder rights.

LEMMA 4.3: The capital stock with shareholder rights is larger than the one without shareholder rights iff

$$\theta \leq \frac{\alpha_{-1}}{\tau_{-1}} \bar{\varphi}_1 + \frac{\bar{\varphi}_0 \left[1 + r - (1 - \bar{\varphi}_1)(1 + a)\right]}{(1 - \bar{\varphi}_0)(1 + a)} \equiv \theta^* \tag{4.9}$$

The intuition is the following: With shareholder rights, the maximum capital stock is also restrained if θ is larger than some level of management ownership needed to remain in control, θ^{**} (which is derived in appendix B, where it is also shown that θ^{**} is always smaller than θ^*). This time the restriction on the capital stock comes from management's desire to remain in control. The income of management equals

$$[\bar{\varphi}_0 + \frac{\alpha_{-1}}{\tau_{-1}}(1 - \bar{\varphi}_0)]\Pi(K_{-1}),$$

i.e. the amount it steals in period 0, $\bar{\varphi}_0$, plus its share of the remaining profits, multiplied by $(1 + r)$ to account for its value in period 1. For every unit of new capital management has to purchase shares with a (period 1) value of $\theta(1 + a)$ to remain in control. However, it owns already $\frac{\alpha_{-1}}{\tau_{-1}}$ shares. These go up in value with an increase in the amount of capital, but not by the full amount of the returns, but by $a - r$, since new investors obtain $1 + r$. The difference between the two represents the resources needed by management to remain in control with every additional unit of capital. If the restriction on control is binding the maximum capital stock corresponds to

$$K_0^{SR} = \frac{[\bar{\varphi}_0 + \frac{\alpha_{-1}}{\tau_{-1}}(1 - \bar{\varphi}_0)]\Pi(K_{-1})(1 + r)}{\theta(1 + a) - \frac{\alpha_{-1}}{\tau_{-1}}(a - r)} \tag{4.10}$$

If $\theta < \theta^{**}$ (i.e. if the stake management needs to control the firm is rather small), every unit of increase in K increases the value of the shares management already holds by an amount which is sufficient to buy up additional shares to remain in control even after the new shares have been issued. In this situation management can reach K^*.

A comparison of K_0^{SR} and K_0^{NR} results in inequality 4.9. One of the crucial parameters of the inequality is $\bar{\varphi}_0$, the amount that can be stolen in period 0. The amount that is stolen in period 0 cannot be added to the capital stock if no shareholder rights are introduced. Therefore it cannot be used to back new finance and has to be consumed in period 0. However, if shareholder rights are in place, the profits stolen in period 0 can be used to acquire new shares for management, relaxing the constraint on the capital stock. Therefore a larger $\bar{\varphi}_0$ increases the capital stock in the presence of shareholder rights. This difference is the more important, the bigger the implicit subsidy $1+r-(1-\bar{\varphi}_1)(1+a)$ management has to use for every new unit of capital in the case of no shareholder rights. It is less important the more management has to pay for the new shares it has to acquire, which depends on $(1+a)$.

Abstracting from this effect (i.e. setting $\bar{\varphi}_0=0$), the share of the firm (post-investment) management must own to remain in control must be sufficiently small (smaller than $\frac{\alpha_{-1}}{\tau_{-1}}$) to allow for a large investment program. With $\gamma_0=0$ it is always the case that management cannot raise any new capital if $\theta > \frac{\alpha_{-1}}{\tau_{-1}}$, because it would always have to buy back some shares in order to remain in control, i.e. to set $s_0 < 0$. Therefore, the capital stock with shareholder rights has to be smaller than the total income of management, i.e. smaller than $\frac{\alpha_{-1}}{\tau_{-1}} \Pi(K_{-1})$. Without shareholder rights, on the other hand, even if $\bar{\varphi}_1$ is very large and therefore the scope to raise new capital is very limited, management could at least invest $\Pi(K_{-1})$. Therefore, the capital stock is always smaller with shareholder rights if $\theta > \frac{\alpha_{-1}}{\tau_{-1}}$. Lastly, the larger the amount of stealing, $\bar{\varphi}_1$, the more likely is it that the capital stock is larger with shareholder rights, since without shareholder rights the amount of old capital necessary to back each unit of new capital is relatively large.

While it is a necessary condition for the introduction of shareholder rights that the capital stock is larger with shareholder rights, it is not a sufficient one, because management might obtain a smaller part of the period 1 profits if it refrains from stealing. The sufficient condition is stated in the following proposition.

PROPOSITION 4.2: Management chooses to introduce shareholder rights iff

$$\theta \leq \frac{(a-r)[\bar{\varphi}_1\,(1+a)-\bar{\varphi}_0\,(a-r)]\frac{\alpha_{-1}}{\tau_{-1}}}{(1+a)(1-\bar{\varphi}_0)[\frac{\alpha_{-1}}{\tau_{-1}}(a-r)+(1-\frac{\alpha_{-1}}{\tau_{-1}})\,\bar{\varphi}_1\,(1+a)]} \equiv \theta^{***} \tag{4.11}$$

and

$$K^* \geq [\frac{\bar{\varphi}_1\,(1+a)}{1+r-(1+a)(1-\bar{\varphi}_1)} - \frac{\alpha_{-1}}{\tau_{-1}}]\frac{(1-\bar{\varphi}_0)(1+r)}{\frac{\alpha_{-1}}{\tau_{-1}}(a-r)}\pi(K_{-1}) \tag{4.12}$$

The interesting condition is condition 4.11, which states, similarly to condition 4.9, that θ must be sufficiently small for management to introduce shareholder rights. The second condition states that K^* must be sufficiently large and is equivalent to $\theta^{**} \leq \theta^{***}$, as can be seen in figure 4.2, which shows that if $\theta^{**}=\theta^{***}, K_0^{SR}=K^*$. In case a) condition 4.12 holds, in case b) it does not. The intuition for condition 4.12 is the following: If K^* is too small, it can be the case that even if K^* can be reached with shareholder rights, management is still worse off, because it can steal less in period 1. Parameters can be such that this is the case, even though $K^* \geq K_0^{NR}$. K^* limits the maximum difference between the capital stock with and without shareholder rights. Given that these differences in capital stocks set the incentives for the introduction of shareholder rights, such rights are never going to be introduced if the difference between the capital stocks cannot be sufficiently large (i.e. if condition 4.12 does not hold).

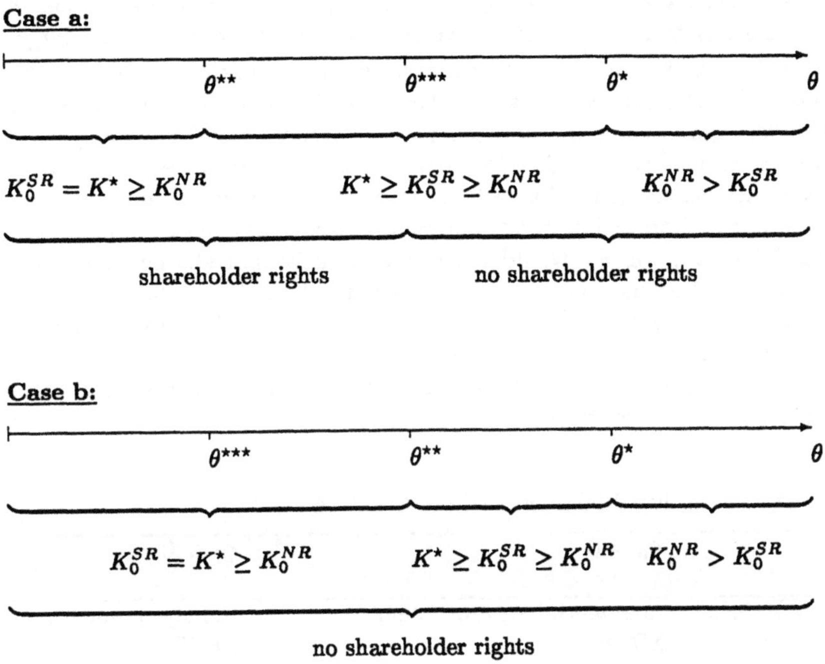

Fig. 4.2. Relative Size of Capital Stocks and Controlling Stakes

The intuition of condition 4.11 is very similar to the one of differences in the capital stock. This is not very surprising, since the only force working in favour of the introduction of shareholder rights is a larger capital stock. Again, the larger $\bar{\varphi}_0$, the more likely is it that shareholder rights will be introduced ($\frac{\partial \theta^{***}}{\partial \bar{\varphi}_0} > 0$). This is the 'money-laundering' case: since the model does not allow the manager to add the profit stolen in period 0 to the capital stock (and leverage it by the new capital raised), they might introduce shareholder rights.

An easy way to abstract from this effect is to set $\bar{\varphi}_0 = 0$, which results in

$$\theta \leq \frac{(a-r)\,\bar{\varphi}_1\,\frac{\alpha_{-1}}{\tau_{-1}}}{\frac{\alpha_{-1}}{\tau_{-1}}(a-r)+(1-\frac{\alpha_{-1}}{\tau_{-1}})\,\bar{\varphi}_1\,(1+a)} \tag{4.13}$$

This is the case of 'managerial entrenchment', where management already owns a sufficient amount of shares. For this case it is again necessary that θ must be smaller than $\frac{\alpha_{-1}}{\tau_{-1}}$ - for the same reason as above. If it is too large, management has to spend too many resources on acquiring further shares. It is also still true that the larger $\bar{\varphi}_1$ the more likely is the introduction of shareholder rights, since in the absence of shareholder rights management needs more capital to subsidize the new shareholders. However, this is only the case because the game has a last period. If it was an infinite game dilution would be impossible because investors would anticipate to be diluted as well. Then a larger $\bar{\varphi}_1$ would make it less likely that shareholder rights are introduced because the implicit transfer to the old shareholders would be the larger, the more can be stolen. This effect is picked up in Chapter 3. Furthermore, shareholder rights are more likely to be introduced if a is large and r is small. This is true as these parameter values translate a larger capital stock into larger profits[8].

Table 4.1. Shareholder Rights in the Two Period Case

	$\phi_0 = 0$	$\phi_0 > 0$
$(1-\phi_1)(1+a)$ $< (1+r)$	managerial entrenchment SR iff $\theta \leq \frac{(a-r)\bar{\phi}_1(1+a)\frac{\alpha_{-1}}{\tau_{-1}}}{(1+a)[\frac{\alpha_{-1}}{\tau_{-1}}(a-r)+(1-\frac{\alpha_{-1}}{\tau_{-1}})\bar{\phi}_1(1+a)]}$	money- laundering SR iff $\theta \leq \theta^{***}$
$(1-\bar{\phi}_1)(1+a)$ $> (1+r)$	excess probitability NSR	excess profitability NSR

To summarize the two-period case, there are two reasons why management might introduce shareholder rights. In the case of 'money-laundering', management might steal a substantial part of period 0 profits and has no other

[8] With a logarithmic utility function the condition under which it is optimal to introduce shareholder rights is more restrictive, whenever management has to acquire further shares to stay in control. These acquisitions lead to a depressed consumption in the first period, boosting consumption in the second. With a logarithmic utility, this effect works against the introduction of shareholder rights.

way to add this money back to the capital stock. Indeed, one would hope that management has some problems 'laundering' its stolen money. Balance of payments data for Russia indicates that flight capital has not yet returned and kept leaving the country even in 1997. At the same time there were large capital inflows from foreign investors, attracted by very high yields. This might partly be due to the difficulties involved in laundering stolen money. However, it is presumably also linked to the attempt by Russian investors to diversify their asset holdings in order to reduce the risk. Second, in the case of 'managerial entrenchment' shareholder rights are introduced by management in case they had exogenously (through privatisation) received enough shares to keep control even after the introduction of shareholder rights. This does not mean that management does not acquire further shares. In general, management would use all its period 0 income to buy further shares to keep control after the new share issue. Nevertheless, management must own some minimum amount of shares from the outset. Furthermore, in case projects are excessively profitable, shareholder rights might not be introduced, simply because projects can also be financed without them.

To explain why management in some firms finds it profitable to introduce shareholder rights even without management owning a controlling stake from the outset and abstracting from the case of money laundering, the implications of increasing the time horizon need to be investigated.

4.3 The Three Period Game

The aim of analysing a three-period game is to show that in a multi-period framework, management might introduce shareholder rights, even if the privatisation procedure has allocated less than θ % of the shares to management and 'money-laundering' is possible.

In a first step the game in the third period is described. In the next section, the set-up of the two-period game is generalized to allow for 'money-laundering'. Previously, the fact that money-laundering was not possible provided one reason for the introduction of shareholder rights. Allowing for money laundering to take place therefore helps to focus on a new case in which shareholder rights are introduced in a multi-period setting, the so-called 'commitment case'. The conditions for this case to hold are derived in section 4.3.1.

In order to focus on the 'commitment case' this section abstracts from the 'managerial entrenchment' case. This is done by analysing an extreme situation, where the share ownership of management at the beginning of period -1, $(\frac{\alpha_{-2}}{\tau_{-2}})$, is set to 0, i.e. a case where management has not received any shares in the privatisation procedure. Furthermore, throughout this section, it is still assumed that $(1+r) > (1-\bar{\varphi}_t)(1+a)$ for period 0 as well as for period 1. This eliminates the case of 'excess profitability'. Lastly, it will be assumed that K^* is larger than the maximum capital stock in period 1 with as well as without shareholder rights.

When adding a period -1 to the game analysed above, the time line remains the same as in the two-period game except that management can also set action parameters in period -1. In particular, management can introduce shareholder rights either in period -1 for period 0 or in period 0 for period 1. In period -1 management obtains income $\bar{\varphi}_{-1}\ \Pi(K_{-2})$ because it does not own any shares initially. It allocates that income between consumption C_{-1} and increasing its share ownership from 0 to α_{-1}. Management also sets dividends in this period, γ_{-1}, and determines the number of new shares issued, s_{-1}. With respect to the introduction of shareholder rights, management has three possible strategies. First, management can choose not to introduce shareholder rights ever, i.e. it will steal in all periods ($\varphi_0 = \bar{\varphi}_0, \varphi_1 = \bar{\varphi}_1$). Second, it can introduce shareholder rights in period -1, which implies that shareholder rights will be honoured as well in the subsequent periods ($\varphi_0 = \varphi_1 = 0$). Third, it can keep stealing in period 0, but introduces shareholder rights for the last period ($\varphi_0 = \bar{\varphi}_0, \varphi_1 = 0$).

If management is to benefit from the last strategy, it is essential that investors believe that shareholder rights will indeed be honoured in the next period. Only then do share-prices reflect this future change in behaviour. This would allow management to sell shares in period -1, backed by the full amount of profits in period 1. The way to commit to a delayed introduction of shareholder rights in the following period is for management to buy up a sufficient amount of shares, such that it is optimal to introduce shareholder rights in period 1. This requires that $\frac{\alpha_{-1}}{\tau_{-1}}$ is large enough for condition 4.11 to hold. If this condition is violated, investors will anticipate that shareholder rights will not be introduced in the following period either.

4.3.1 Allowing for Money-Laundering

Since this section of the chapter aims to abstract from the case where shareholder rights are introduced because money-laundering is not possible, the set-up is now slightly modified and management is allowed to re-invest its stolen profits. As the three-period model is to be solved by backward induction, this section first derives how this change affects the strategies in the two-period model (or, to be more precise, in the last two periods of the three-period model). In particular, a new condition for the minimum management share ownership for the introduction of shareholder rights is derived. Allowing for money laundering only affects the outcome in the absence of shareholder rights, since only then is management forced to consume a positive amount ($\bar{\varphi}_0\ \pi(K_{-1})$) in period 0 instead of reinvesting it. Therefore, the capital stock in the absence of shareholder rights changes when money laundering is allowed. This section also derives this capital stock.

Allowing for money-laundering makes the introduction of shareholder rights less likely in the two-period set-up and condition 4.11 for the introduction of shareholder rights in period 0 consequently becomes stricter. If what had previously been consumed in period 0 is added to the capital stock K_0 instead, the capital stock in period 1 is $\frac{\pi(K_{-1})}{1-\frac{(1-\bar{\varphi}_1)(1+a)}{1+r}}$, resulting in consumption of $\bar{\varphi}_1\ (1+a)\frac{\pi(K_{-1})}{1-\frac{(1-\bar{\varphi}_1)(1+a)}{1+r}}$. Given that consumption under shareholder rights remains as previously analysed, condition 4.11 is now replaced by

$$\frac{\alpha_{-1}}{\tau_{-2}+s_{-1}} \geq \frac{\theta[\bar{\varphi}_1\ (1+a) - \bar{\varphi}_0\ [(1+r)-(1+a)(1-\bar{\varphi}_1)]}{\theta(1-\bar{\varphi}_0)[(1+r)-(1+a)(1-\bar{\varphi}_1)] + \bar{\varphi}_1\ (a-r)} \equiv \left(\frac{\alpha_{-1}}{\tau_{-1}}\right)^* \tag{4.14}$$

Only if condition 4.14 holds, it is credible that management will introduce shareholder rights for period 1. If it does not hold and management does not introduce shareholder rights in period -1, investors anticipate that there won't be shareholder rights in the following periods either. With the possibility of money laundering, the capital stock in the three-period game is given by the following Lemma.

LEMMA 4.4: If condition 4.14 does not hold and if management does not introduce shareholder rights for period 0 and money laundering is possible, the capital stock at the end of period 0 is

$$K_0^{NSR} = \frac{(1+a)\Pi(K_{-2})}{1-\frac{(1-\bar{\varphi}_1)(1+a)}{(1+r)}}, \tag{4.15}$$

In the first period the maximum capital stock in the absence of shareholder rights is restricted to the level of income the manager obtains from the firm. In this repeated game it is not possible to use the existing capital to secure new investment (by diluting the existing shareholders) since the potential new shareholders anticipate to be diluted in the next round. Only in the second round is dilution going to take place. Therefore, the capital stock increases by only $(1+a)$ in the first period.

4.3.2 Conditions for Introduction of Shareholder Rights

This section compares the different strategies in a three-period set-up. First, the strategy of introducing shareholder rights immediately ($\varphi_0 = 0, \varphi_1 = 0$) is compared with the strategy of never introducing shareholder rights ($\varphi_0 = \bar{\varphi}_0$, $\varphi_1 = \bar{\varphi}_1$). It turns out that the latter is always superior given the assumptions introduced above. In the next step the commitment strategy ($\varphi_0 = \bar{\varphi}_0, \varphi_1 = 0$) is compared with the strategy of never introducing shareholder rights ($\varphi_0 = \bar{\varphi}_0, \varphi_1 = \bar{\varphi}_1$).

First, comparing the introduction of shareholder rights already in the first period with the situation of never introducing shareholder rights results in the following proposition:

PROPOSITION 4.3: With $\frac{\alpha_{-2}}{\tau_{-2}} = 0$ and if money laundering is possible, management never introduces shareholder rights in period -1 in the three-period game.

Although management in the absence of shareholder rights cannot raise capital by diluting existing outside shareholders, it is still the case that shareholder rights will never be introduced when allowing for money-laundering and excluding large initial ownership by management. It can even be shown that the increase in the capital stock due to adding a third period is larger if there are no shareholder rights in either period, than if shareholder rights are implemented in both periods. The intuition is the following: without shareholder rights, there is no share issue in the first period, but all profits $\pi(K_{-2})$ are re-invested in the firm. This will result in profits of $(1+a)\pi(K_{-2})$ in the following period. This capital stock is then used to raise new capital by diluting existing shareholders. When comparing the two- and the three-period case, the capital stock rises by $(1+a)$ due to the additional period. With shareholder rights, the capital stock of period -1 also rises by $(1+a)$, but at the same time, shares of the firm become more expensive by the factor $\frac{1+a}{1+r}$. As a result, management's wealth becomes a stricter constraint and the capital stock rises by less than $(1+a)$ when adding a third period. Given that the only reason for the introduction of shareholder rights is a potentially larger capital stock, this implies shareholder rights will never be introduced in the three-period case if they are not implemented in the two-period case. Because the analysis for the three-period case abstracts from the two cases that led to the introduction of shareholder rights in the two-period game, this must mean that shareholder rights are never introduced in this three-period setting.

It is more interesting to analyse the case where management commits to introduce shareholder rights in the subsequent period by purchasing a sufficient amount of shares in period -1. The next proposition compares the strategy of never introducing shareholder rights ($\varphi_0 = \bar{\varphi}_0, \varphi_1 = \bar{\varphi}_1$) with the strategy to commit to a delayed introduction ($\varphi_0 = 0, \varphi_1 = \bar{\varphi}_1$):

PROPOSITION 4.4 (Commitment Case): Management does commit to introduce shareholder rights for period 1 by purchasing $\frac{\alpha_{-1}}{\tau_{-2}+s_{-1}} = \left(\frac{\alpha_{-1}}{\tau_{-1}}\right)^*$ shares in period -1, if

$$\bar{\varphi}_{-1}\,(1+r)^2 + \bar{\varphi}_0\,(1+a)(1+r) \geq \frac{\bar{\varphi}_1\,(1+a)^2}{1-\frac{(1+a)(1-\bar{\varphi}_1)}{1+r}} \tag{4.16}$$

The costs of the commitment strategy are the following: for large $\left(\frac{\alpha_{-1}}{\tau_{-1}}\right)^*$, management needs considerable resources in order to convince investors that shareholder rights will be introduced in the next period by buying up a sufficient amount of shares. This keeps the capital stock at the end of period -1 rather small and reduces consumption at the end of period 1. To clarify the benefits of the commitment strategy the equilibrium in which all period

0 profits are paid out as dividends is analysed. For a given capital stock at the end of the game, share-prices under the commitment strategy are lower than if shareholder rights are introduced immediately, because $\bar{\varphi}_0$ % of period 0 profits are stolen. Furthermore, these stolen profits are then used to buy up shares such that management can issue additional shares without losing control. Stealing in period -1 can therefore increase the amount of capital management can raise without losing control. The smaller a and the larger r, the cheaper are the shares and the easier it is for management to buy up a sufficient stake in order to commit to the introduction of shareholder rights. The sign of the derivatives with respect to a and r are different from the ones in the two-period case. The reason is that in the three-period case management has to acquire θ% of shares. Therefore, the price of the shares constrain management's capability to raise new capital while remaining in control. The shareprice is higher, the larger a and the smaller r. In the two-period case, management might own a sufficiently large stake in the firm from the outset. Then its wealth increases the larger a, since a large a relaxes the constraint on the capital expenditure program. Furthermore, the larger $\bar{\varphi}_1$, the more binding the constraint in the absence of shareholder rights, because more existing capital is necessary to back the new shares.

Another way to interpret inequality 4.16 is to note that if multiplied by $\pi(K_{-2})$, the right hand side would equal consumption at the end of period 1 in the absence of shareholder rights. The left hand side would then be the terminal value of income management obtains in period -1 and 0. Management invests $\bar{\varphi}_{-1}\ \pi(K_{-2})$ in shares in period -1 and $\bar{\varphi}_0\ (1+a)\pi(K_{-2})$ in shares in period 0. Since the shares result in return r per period, the left hand side of condition 4.16 is the amount management can consume in period 1. If that amount is larger than consumption in the absence of shareholder rights, such rights will be introduced. If management can steal for one more period, it decreases the value of the shares of existing shareholders. This decreases the size of the transfer to the existing shareholders in case shareholder rights are introduced. The larger $\bar{\varphi}_0$, the more likely is it that the transfer to existing shareholders by introducing shareholder rights are more than compensated for by the larger capital stock.

It is noteworthy that the introduction of shareholder rights does not depend on total wealth of management, i.e. on its period -1 income ($\bar{\varphi}_{-1}$ $\pi(K_{-2})$), but only on $\bar{\varphi}_{-1}$. Higher profits at the outset, i.e. larger $\pi(K_{-2})$, increase management's wealth, but also increase the extent to which the firm can finance itself without the introduction of shareholders rights. However, if management can increase its income by stealing a larger proportion of profits (i.e. a higher $\bar{\varphi}_{-1}$), management is more likely to introduce shareholder rights.

4.4 Social Welfare

It is clear that a social planner would allocate enough capital to the firm that it can reach K^* in the first period. Without shareholder rights, K^* is in general not reached because outsiders are unwilling to fund the new project, as part of its returns will be stolen. With shareholder rights, this level might not be reached because management wants to stay in control. This results in an inefficiently low capital stock. Even if management commits to refrain from stealing (by introducing shareholder rights) the efficient capital stock is in general still not reached, because this commitment might result in a loss of private benefits of control. As those benefits are not contractible, the first best outcome is in general not achieved.

Apart from the inefficiency mentioned above, there is a second inefficiency. It could be the case that the capital stock with shareholder rights is smaller than K^* , but larger than the capital stock without shareholder rights. Nevertheless, management might choose not to introduce shareholder rights, such that even the second best is not reached. This can happen because of a free-rider situation, similar to *Grossman and Hart (1980)*. If shareholder rights are not introduced the shares of the existing investors are worthless. If investors transfered these shares to management, shareholder rights might be introduced so that the shares would become valuable. Every (atomistic) shareholder does not take into account that its action changes the probability that shareholder rights are introduced and therefore does not tender the shares. As a result, shareholder rights are not introduced.

The obvious policy conclusion would be to give a majority of shares to management at the outset of the privatisation procedure. Alternatively, dual-class shares could offer a solution, where the shares management obtains carry more voting rights than other shares. Both policies would shorten the period of time it takes until management introduces shareholder rights. Both policy conclusions have been implemented in Russia only up to a point. On the one hand, preference shares have been issued to employees in many firms, amounting in general to 25% of charter capital. This would facilitate it for management to keep control of the firm after the introduction of shareholder rights, as only 50% of the shares that carry a voting premium have to be acquired. On the other hand, management ownership directly after the privatisation program fell significantly short of the levels required for management to remain in control after the introduction of shareholder rights. *Blasi* (1994) reports that top management held on average only 9% of shares (which presumably includes non-voting shares, though). Policy makers had apparently decided that the post-privatisation ownership of management should only be limited. In particular, it can be argued that significant management ownership is detrimental to restructuring in case it is necessary to replace management, which often lacks the necessary skills to operate in a market economy. *Barberis et al (1995)* present some evidence from Russian privatized retail shops that restructuring was not significantly correlated with management's incentive schemes, but strongly with new management. *Johnson and Loveman (1995)* obtain similar conclusions from Polish case studies. However, it is *a priori* not clear whether this means that management should own only few shares. On the one hand, if management owns a lot of shares, it is harder to replace it against its will. However, management would also gain more from improved efficiency as a major shareholder. In any case, this chapter focuses on an environment where the state is not strong enough to enforce rules that could force management out of its job. Some evidence for this assumption has been given earlier in this chapter and in the introduction for the case of Russia. This chapter demonstrates that in that case it can be better if management consolidates its control quickly instead of letting the consolidation happen over a long period of time which depresses investment. The weakness of the state was presumably not sufficiently taken into account when the privatisation process had been devised.

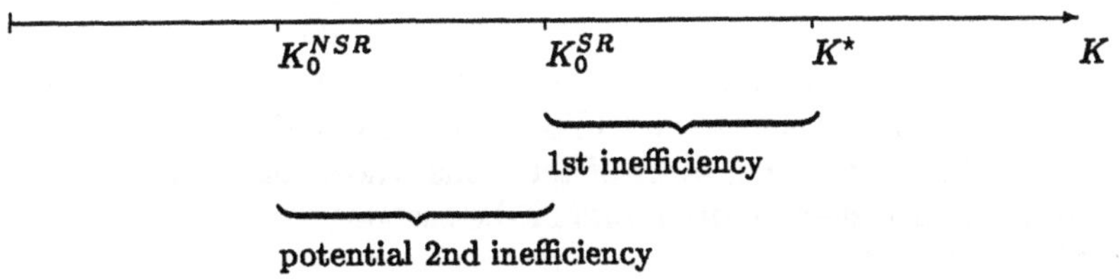

Fig. 4.3. Two Inefficiencies

4.5 Conclusion

The conclusions of the model are that there are market forces which push management towards the voluntary introduction of shareholder rights even in the absence of state guaranteed shareholder rights, but that this process will in most cases take a considerable amount of time to work. While there are cases where a larger capital stock can be reached once shareholder rights have been introduced, this is not always the case in an environment where management wants to stay in control of the firm. For example, if projects are so profitable that they can be financed in spite of the fact that management steals part of the profits, forces which work towards the introduction of shareholder rights are weak. Also, if management does not own a sufficient amount of shares at the outset, which makes it prohibitively expensive to buy up enough shares for management to remain in control, in equilibrium no shareholder rights are introduced in the short run. Lastly, if 'money-laundering' is possible, i.e. if the profits stolen can be used to increase the firm's capital stock, this would also weaken the incentives to introduce shareholder rights in the short run. However, in a three-period model more firms introduce shareholder rights, but only after they have stolen enough profits (and invested them in the firm) that they are not going to lose control by introducing shareholder rights.

While a third period is sufficient to show that management might introduce shareholder rights once it has diminished the value of the claims of the old shareholders, it is interesting to analyse the introduction of additional periods. Interpreting the last period as the period where firms have completed their capital expenditure program, new periods are added before period -1, i.e. period -2 etc. Allowing for such periods results in more firms introducing shareholder rights. The reason is the following: one strategy for management (not necessarily the optimal one) would be to steal some profits in a previous period (i.e. period -2) and to invest them in the firm. Then the extra period would change nothing in the set-up apart from the fact that management now holds some positive fraction of the shares at the beginning of period -1. Therefore, the constraint on capital formation in the presence of shareholder rights is less binding and some additional firms would introduce shareholder rights. At the same time, some of the firms whose management is committed to introduce shareholder rights in the second period of the three-period game will commit to introduce such rights already in the second period of the four-period game. However, management of some other firms might commit to introduce such rights only in the third period. This is true, because it has been shown in proposition 4.3 that firms which do *not* introduce shareholder rights for the last period, will never introduce them for the last two periods. However, some firms which do introduce shareholder rights for the last period, might not introduce them for the last two periods. This implies that the stake management must acquire in the first period in order to commit to introduce shareholder rights in the following period is likely to be larger for the four-period game than for the three-period game. Therefore, management of some firms could find it profitable to delay the introduction of shareholder rights by one period. The underlying reason is that shares become more expensive when another period is added. Then the ownership constraint on the capital stock with shareholder rights becomes stricter for a given level of management ownership. Lastly, if there was no last period, the introduction of shareholder rights would be more likely. This is true as there can be no infinite dilution in the absence of shareholder rights because no-one would buy the shares, fearing a dilution in the subsequent period. This would reduce the potential capital stock with shareholder rights and therefore increase the likelihood of the introduction of shareholder rights. It also would imply that it is not true that firms, where a large share of profits can be stolen, are more likely to introduce shareholder rights. After all, the size of the subsidy such firms would need to pay to attract new capital would go to infinity, independent of $\bar{\varphi}_1$. Then the other effect, that giving up a larger benefit from stealing entails a larger transfer to existing shareholders, would be dominant. Therefore, firms where only a small fraction of profits can be stolen would be more likely to introduce shareholder rights.

The model generates a number of testable predictions, the most important of which is that managers might introduce shareholder rights even in the absence of state enforced laws on these issues, but in most cases not immediately. Furthermore, there are some testable hypotheses of interest from the comparative statics of the propositions derived above: First, firms which do not introduce shareholder rights should not pay any dividends[9]. This would be consistent with the finding of chapter 3 that large firms (with a possibly smaller expected value of stealing) are more likely to pay dividends. However, dividend payments are not positively linked to the introduction of shareholder rights. This might be due to particularities in the institutional context of Russia (see chapter 3). However, on a more general level, studies in developed markets find that dividend payments are at times used to signal good information, possibly about the type of management[10]. This would be broadly consistent with this model. Second, if management does not introduce shareholder rights, it might choose to dilute existing shareholders. Dilutions have indeed occurred in Russia, the most recent case being the oil subsidiaries of SiDanCo. However, a detailed study of how these dilutions interact with the introduction of shareholder rights has not been carried out so far. Third, shareholder rights are more likely to be introduced (or more quickly introduced) in firms where management owns a large portion of the shares from the privatisation procedure, or where a large part of profits can be stolen in the direct aftermath of privatisation (high $\bar{\varphi}_{-1}, \bar{\varphi}_0$), such that it can quickly buy up more shares. Significant potential for stealing in the periods close to the end of the capital expenditure program ($\bar{\varphi}_1$) would make the introduction of shareholder rights less likely. The amount of share ownership by management would presumably be in excess of the moderate ownership advocated by *Jensen and Meckling (1976)* to mitigate the standard agency problems. Unfortunately, there is no reliable data on ownership of managers

---

[9] If the model was extended to include some uncertainty (i.e. over how much can be stolen in a given firm), the payment of dividends could be used to signal to investors that the potential for stealing is limited.

[10] For theoretical models, see *Bhattarchaya (1980)* and for empirical evidence, for example, *Asquith and Mullins (1983)*.

Furthermore, *Ravid and Sudit (1994)* present a model where dividend payments ensure that inefficiencies due to power seeking managers are mitigated.

for the firms that are actively traded. However, *Earle and Estrin (1996)* find that it is in particular management ownership which spurs increases in productivity as well as long-term restructuring. Given that access to new capital, which is clearly necessary for restructuring to occur, is limited in the absence of shareholder rights, their evidence would be somewhat supportive of my hypothesis. Also, *Blasi et al (1997)* provide some evidence that management is indeed buying up shares from workers. In their sample of small and medium sized firms insiders owned in 1996 58% of shares, down from 65% in 1994. Top management held 10%, up from 7% directly after the privatisation in 1994. In a separate question, management professed on average to aim for ownership of 50%. Lastly, the smaller the amount of shares needed to control a firm, the more likely is the introduction of shareholder rights. This hypothesis could be tested by analysing in detail corporate charters. If management never requires 75% of votes for any actions, it should be more likely to introduce shareholder rights than managers in firms which do require such a majority for many decisions.

4.6 Appendix A

Table 4.2. Definition of Variables

C_t	Consumption of management, period t
P_t	Private benefits of management, period t
K_t	Capital stock, end of period t
γ_t	Dividend pay-out ratio, period t
S_t	Number of new shares issued, period t
α_t	Number of shares owned by management, period t
τ_t	Number of outstanding shares, period t
ϕ_t	Profits stolen in period t, set in period t-1
a	Return on projects
r	Required return
p_t	Share price, period t

4.7 Appendix B

4.7.1 Proof of Lemma 4.1

It is clear that in case of a two-period model, the dividend payout ratio for the second period, γ_1, is set to 1 since there is no need to maintain a capital stock for the future. Furthermore, the dividend-payout ratio in period 0, γ_0, can optimally be set equal to 0. This is a direct result of the linearity of the utility function. Since management earns a higher return than required ($a > r$) if the profit of period 0 is used to increase the capital stock (and not for consumption) and since there is no gain from consumption smoothing, management always sets C_0 to 0 as long as the resulting capital stock is smaller than K^*. Without shareholder rights, where the ability to raise outside capital might be restricted because of stealing, the capital stock is largest if no dividends are paid out. With shareholder rights, the capital stock might be restricted by the fact that management wants to remain in control and has to buy up shares to achieve this aim. Since it buys up these shares with its period 0 cash-flows, one might be tempted to believe that this might require that the optimal dividend payout ratio is positive. However, positive dividends are never necessary to reach the optimal capital stock, since there are two instruments, γ_0 as well as the amount of shares issues, s_0. Only one of these two variables is necessary to reach the optimal capital stock if shareholder rights have been introduced. If a positive dividend is paid out, management can buy up more shares and therefore the share issue can be larger without management losing control. However, the capital stock is decreased by the fact that part of last period's profits are paid out instead of being added to the capital stock. The two effects exactly offset each other. It is therefore never sub-optimal to set $\gamma_0 = 0$ if shareholder rights were introduced[11].□

4.7.2 Proof of Proposition 4.1

In case $(1-\bar{\varphi}_1)(1+a) < (1+r)$ the post-stealing return of the investment is large enough to cover the required rate of return for the new investors. Therefore, management can raise any required capital stock even in the absence of shareholder rights. Given the above profit function it is clear that in the absence of shareholder rights it is always optimal to set $K_0 = K^*$. On the other hand, the capital stock with shareholder rights might be smaller than K^* as the number of new shares to be issued is restricted by management's desire to stay in control (see Lemma 4.4). Therefore, if the capital stock without shareholder rights is not constrained by stealing, the capital stock with shareholder rights will always be smaller. This makes it suboptimal to introduce shareholder rights[12].□

4.7.3 Proof of Lemma 4.2

If $(1-\bar{\varphi}_1)(1+a) < (1+r)$ from equations 4.4, 4.5, 4.6 and 4.7 it follows that

$$K_0 = \frac{(1-\gamma_0)(1-\bar{\varphi}_0)\Pi(K_{-1})}{1-\frac{s_0(1-\bar{\varphi}_1)(1+a)}{(\tau_{-1}+s_0)(1+r)}}, \tag{4.17}$$

which is maximized as s_0 goes to infinity and $\gamma_0 = 0$. The capital stock in the absence of shareholder rights is then

$$K_0^{NR} = \frac{(1-\bar{\varphi}_0)\Pi(K_{-1})(1+r)}{1+r-(1-\bar{\varphi}_1)(1+a)} \tag{4.18}$$

[11] In case there are insufficient funds for purchasing new shares to remain in control with the introduction of shareholder rights, there has to be a buy-back of shares, such that management can remain in control even with shareholder rights, in spite of the limited cash-flow in period 0.

[12] This result is so clear-cut because of the linearity of the profit function. With a concave profit function the first-best level for the capital stock would in general not be reached in the absence of shareholder rights.

In case management does not find it advantageous to introduce shareholder rights, it profits most from this increased capital stock (the new investors only obtain a return r, smaller than the return of the new assets, a, and the old investors receive nothing in case s_0 goes to infinity), management is better off the larger K_0, as long as $K^* > K_0$. □

4.7.4 Proof of Lemma 4.3

With shareholder rights two cases need to be distinguished. If

$$\theta \leq \frac{(a-r)\frac{\alpha_{-1}}{\tau_{-1}}}{1+a} + [\bar{\varphi}_0 + \frac{\alpha_{-1}}{\tau_{-1}}(1-\bar{\varphi}_0)](1+r)\frac{K_{-1}}{K^*} \equiv \theta^{**} \tag{4.19}$$

there is no restriction on the capital stock and management then sets $K_0 = K^*$. This is true since for every unit of increase in K the value of the shares management already holds in period 0 increases by an amount which is sufficient to buy up the extra shares to remain in control even after new shares have been issued to fund the extra unit of K. If $\theta \leq \theta^{**}$ and K^* is larger than K_0^{NR}, it is obvious that the capital stock with shareholder rights is larger than without. In this case it is also in general true that management can in addition afford to consume something in period 0 without decreasing the capital stock.

If $\theta > \theta^{**}$, the capital stock in the presence of shareholder rights is restricted by the fact that management wants to remain in control. The more shares it has to buy in period 0, the less it can consume in this period. Since returns to investment, a, are higher than required returns, r, which are used to discount period 1 utility, it is optimal for management to set consumption in period 0 to zero, if K^* is sufficiently large. The resulting capital stock for period 1 is then

$$K_0^{SR} = \frac{[\bar{\varphi}_0 + \frac{\alpha_{-1}}{\tau_{-1}}(1-\bar{\varphi}_0)]\Pi(K_{-1})(1+r)}{\theta(1+a) - \frac{\alpha_{-1}}{\tau_{-1}}(a-r)} \tag{4.20}$$

which is independent of γ_0 and s_0, as there is an infinite amount of combinations of these two variables to reach K_0^{SR}. K_0^{NR} is smaller than K_0^{SR} if the inequality 4.9 holds. Given that $(1-\bar{\varphi}_1)(1+a) < (1+r)$ and $K^* \geq K_0^{NR}$ condition 4.19 always holds if condition 4.9 does. It follows that $\theta^{**} \leq \theta^*$. Therefore, $K_0^{SR} > K_0^{NSR}$ iff condition 4.9 holds.□

4.7.5 Proof of Proposition 4.2

It can be shown that condition 4.12 is equivalent to the condition $\theta^{**} \leq \theta^{***}$. Assuming that this condition holds, consumption in period 0 with shareholder rights is zero and $\theta(1+a)K_0^{SR}$ in period 1. In the absence of shareholder rights, consumption amounts to $\bar{\varphi}_0 \; \Pi(K_{-1})$ in period 0 and $\bar{\varphi}_1 \; (1+a)K_0^{NR}$ in period 1. Comparing the present value of the pay-offs of both strategies results in the inequality 4.11. However, if $\theta^{**} \geq \theta^{***}$ (i.e. condition 4.12 does not hold) the capital stock with shareholder rights for values of $\theta < \theta^{***}$ would be larger than K^*, which is never optimal due to the shape of the profit function. Therefore, if condition 4.12 does not hold, the capital stock will be K^* and shareholder rights are never introduced.□

4.7.6 Proof of Lemma 4.4

Given the analysis of the strategy management plays in the last two periods of the game, it is clear that if condition 4.14 does not hold and if management does not introduce shareholder rights in period 0, it will dilute all existing shareholders in period 1. Furthermore, there are no dividends going to be paid in period 1. This is anticipated by investors. The price at which they are willing to buy shares in period -1 therefore drops to 0. As a result, no new share-issue can take place and $s_{-1} = 0$. Also, management sets dividends γ_{-1} to 0, such that it earns the higher rate of return, a, on that capital. If it is assumed that management can reinvest its stolen profits $\bar{\varphi}_{-1} \; \Pi(K_{-2})$ and consequently does not consume anything in period -1, it earns $(1+a)\%$ on the full period -1 profit and enters period 0 with a profit of $(1+a)\Pi(K_{-2})$. Again, management will then not pay any dividends ($\gamma_0 = 0$) and re-invests the stolen profits $\bar{\varphi}_0 \; (1+a)\Pi(K_{-2})$, which results in $C_0 = 0$. Therefore, the full amount of last period's profits, $(1+a)\Pi(K_{-2})$, can be used to subsidize new capital in the last period.□

4.7.7 Proof of Proposition 4.3

By assumption it is not possible to reverse the process of the introduction of shareholder rights. Therefore, if φ_0 is set to 0, φ_1 must be 0 as well. Since returns to investment, a, are higher than the discount rate, r, it is optimal for management to set consumption in period -1 as well as in period 0 to zero, such that a comparatively large amount of income can be spent on the acquisition of new shares. This results in the following capital stock:

$$K_0^{SR} = \frac{\bar{\varphi}_{-1} \; (1+a)\Pi(K_{-2})(1+r)^2}{\theta(1+a)^2} \tag{4.21}$$

Again, the capital stock at period 1, K_1^{SR}, is independent of γ_0 and s_0, as well as of γ_{-1} and s_{-1}, as there is an infinite amount of combinations for each pair of variables. It is straightforward to see that consumption with shareholder rights, $\theta(1+a)K_0^{SR}$, is always smaller than consumption in the absence of shareholder rights, $\bar{\varphi}_1 \; (1+a)K_0^{NSR}$.□

4.7.8 Proof of Proposition 4.4

If management does not introduce shareholder rights in period -1, but commits to do so for period 0, the capital stock is

$$K_0^{SR2} = \frac{\bar{\varphi}_{-1}\left[\bar{\varphi}_0 + \left(\frac{\alpha_{-1}}{\tau_{-1}}\right)^*(1-\bar{\varphi}_0)\right](1+a)\Pi(K_{-2})(1+r)^2}{\left(\frac{\alpha_{-1}}{\tau_{-1}}\right)^*\left[(a-r)(1+a)\,\bar{\varphi}_0 + (1-\bar{\varphi}_0)(1+a)^2\theta\right]} \tag{4.22}$$

This is the case because management sets $\frac{\alpha_{-1}}{\tau_{-2}+s_{-1}} = \left(\frac{\alpha_{-1}}{\tau_{-1}}\right)^*$. To commit to introduce shareholder rights in the subsequent period, management needs to fulfil condition 4.14. It would never choose to set $\frac{\alpha_{-1}}{\tau_{-2}+s_{-1}} > \left(\frac{\alpha_{-1}}{\tau_{-1}}\right)^*$, as this would restrict the capital stock at the end of period -1 even further. Therefore, it would set $\frac{\alpha_{-1}}{\tau_{-2}+s_{-1}} = \left(\frac{\alpha_{-1}}{\tau_{-1}}\right)^*$. When management announces the acquisition of $\left(\frac{\alpha_{-1}}{\tau_{-1}}\right)^*$ shares, investors realize that management will introduce shareholder rights in the next period and that dilution will not occur. Therefore, the shareprice in period -1 is positive. Focusing on the equilibrium with zero dividend payments (which is only one out of an infinite amount of pay-off equivalent equilibria) the shareprice in period -1 is therefore

$$p_{-1} = \frac{(1+a)K_0^{SR2}}{(\tau_{-2}+s_{-1}+s_0)(1+r)^2} \tag{4.23}$$

Since returns to investment, a, are higher than the discount rate, r, it is optimal for management to set consumption in period -1 as well as in period 0 to zero, such that a comparatively large amount of income can be spent on the acquisition of new shares. This results in K_1^{SR2}. Again, the capital stock at period 1, K_1^{SR2}, is independent of γ_0 and s_0, as well as of γ_{-1} and s_{-1}, as there is an infinite amount of combinations for each pair of variables. Condition 4.16 directly follows from comparing $\theta(1+a)K_0^{SR2}$, consumption at the end of period 1 under the strategy $\{\varphi_0 = \bar{\varphi}, \varphi_1 = 0\}$, with $\bar{\varphi}_1\,(1+a)K_0^{NSR}$, consumption under the strategy $\{\varphi_0 = \bar{\varphi}_0, \varphi_1 = \bar{\varphi}_1\}$. If condition 4.16 holds the utility of management is always highest with the strategy $\{\varphi_0 = \bar{\varphi}_0, \varphi_1 = 0\}$.□

List of Figures

2.1 Sequential Privatisation 20

3.1 The Effect of Stealing 55

4.1 The Game Managers Play 94
4.2 Relative Size of Capital Stocks and Controlling Stakes 101
4.3 Two Inefficiencies 109

List of Tables

1.1 World Bank Survey of 439 Industrial Firms, Mid-1994 3
1.2 Survey of 7 Regional Property Funds, August 1994 3
1.3 The Russian National Survey 3
1.4 State Ownership by Percentile 4
1.5 Partial Privatisation in the Oil Industry 5
1.6 Blockholders in Russian Firms 6

3.1 Premia of Ordinary Shares over Preference Shares as Percentage of Ordinary Share Price 58
3.2 Correlation of Indicators of Shareholder Rights 62
3.3 Ownership of Russian Firms 65
3.4 Fall in Output and Change in Prices by Industry 67
3.5 OLS Regressions with L 71
3.6 PROBIT Regressions with L 72
3.7 OLS Regressions without L 74
3.8 PROBIT Regressions without L 75
3.9 PE Regressions 77
3.10 PE Regressions without Index 78
3.11 Correlation Between Issues and Shareholder Rights 79
3.12 List of Variables 82
3.13 Shareholder Rights by Industry 83
3.14 Ownership by Industry 83
3.15 Measures of Association* 84
3.16 OLS Regressions without L^2 84
3.17 PROBIT Regressions without L^2 85
3.18 Three Stage Least Squares Regressions without Index 86

4.1 Shareholder Rights in the Two Period Case 102
4.2 Definition of Variables 113

List of Tables

[illegible]
8.10 [illegible] Significance of Conditional [illegible]
[illegible]

Bibliography

1. Admati, A., Pfleiderer, P., Zechner, A. (1994): Large Shareholder Activism, Risk Sharing and Financial Market Equilibrium. Journal of Political Economy 102/6, 1097-1130
2. Aghion, P., Blanchard O., Burgess, R. (1994): The Behavior of State Firms in Eastern Europe Pre-Privatization. European Economic Review 38, 1327-1349
3. Aghion, P., Bolton, P. (1992): An Incomplete Contracts Approach to Financial Contracting. Review of Economic Studies 59, 473-494
4. Akamatsu, N. (1995): Enterprise Governance and Investment Funds in Russian Privatization. In Aoki, M., Kim, H.-K. (Eds.): Corporate Governance in Transitional Economies: Insider Control and the Role of Banks. EDI Development Studies, World Bank, 121-184
5. Allan, F., Faulhaber, G. (1989): Signalling by Underpricing in the IPO Market. Journal of Financial Economics 23, 303-323
6. Asquith, P., Mullins, D. (1983): The Impact of Initiating Dividends Payments on Shareholders' Wealth. Journal of Business 56, 77-96
7. Barberis, N., Boycko, M., Shleifer, A., Tsukanova, N. (1995): How does Privatization Work ? Evidence from Russian Shops. Harvard University mimeo
8. Bergloef, E. (1995): Corporate Governance in Transition Economies: The Theory and its Policy Implications. In Aoki, M., Kim, H.-K. (Eds.): Corporate Governance in Transition Economies. EDI Development Studies, World Bank, 59-98
9. Bhattarchaya, S. (1979): Imperfect Information, Dividend Policy and 'The Bird in the Hand' Fallacy. Bell Journal of Economics, 1-24
10. Bhattacharya, S. (1980): Nondissipative Signalling Structure and Dividend Policy. Quarterly Journal of Economics 95/1, 1-24

11. Blasi, J. (1994): Corporate Governance in Russia. Paper presented at a joint conference of the World Bank and the Central European University Privatization Project, Washington D.C.
12. Blasi, J., Shleifer, A. (1996): Corporate Ownership and Corporate Governance in the Russian Federation. Research Report of the Federal Commission on the Capital Market
13. Blasi, J., Kroumova, M., Kruse, D. (1997): Kremlin Capitalism: Privatizing the Russian Economy. Cornell University Press
14. Boardman, A., Vining, A. (1989): Ownership and Performance in Competitive Environments: A Comparison of the Performance of Private, Mixed and State-owned Enterprises. Journal of Law and Economics 32/1, 1-33
15. Boes, D. (1991): Privatization: a Theoretical Treatment. Clarendon Press, Oxford
16. Bolton, P., Roland, G. (1992): Privatization Policies in Central and Eastern Europe. Economic Policy 15, 276-309
17. Boone, P., Federov, B. (1997): The Ups and Downs of Russian Economic Reforms. In Parker, S., Sachs, J., Woo, W. (Eds.): Economies in Transition: Comparing Asia and Europe. MIT Press, 161-188
18. Boycko, M., Shleifer, A., Vishny, R. (1992): Privatizing Russia. Brooking Papers of Economic Activity 2, 139-192
19. Boycko, M., Shleifer A., Vishny, R. (1995): Privatizing Russia. MIT Press
20. Brunswick Brokerage (1996, 1997): Equity Handbook
21. Cheung, Y., Shum, C. (1995): International Stock Exchange Listing and the Reduction of Political Risk. Managerial and Decision Economics 16, 537-546
22. Cornelli, F., Li, D. (1995): Large Shareholders, Private Benefits of Control, and Optimal Schemes of Privatization. LBS Working Paper
23. Coopers and Lybrand (1996): A Guide to Russian Accounting, Moscow
24. Demougin, A., Sinn, H.-W. (1992): Privatization, Risk Taking and the Communist Firm. CEPR Discussion Paper 743
25. Dewatripont, M., Roland, G. (1993): The Design of Reform Packages. ECARE mimeo
26. Dewatripont, M., Roland, G. (1995): Transition as a Process of Large-Scale Institutional Change. ECARE mimeo
27. Earle, J., Estrin, S. (1996): Privatization versus Competition: Changing Enterprise Behavior in Russia. Centre for Economic Performance Discussion Paper 316

28. Earle, J., Estrin, S., Leshchenko, L. (1996): Ownership Structures, Patterns of Control and Enterprise Behavior in Russia. In Commander, S., Fan, Q., Schaffer, M. (Eds.): Enterprise Restructuring and Economic Policy in Russia. EDI Development Studies, 205-252
29. Earle, J., Rose, R. (1996): Ownership Transformation, Economic Behavior and Political Attitudes in Russia. LBS mimeo
30. Eaton, J., Gersovitz, M., Stiglitz, J. (1986): The Pure Theory of Country Risk. European Economic Review 30, 418-513
31. Estrin, S. (1994): Privatization in Central and Eastern Europe. Longman
32. Estrin, S., Perotin, V. (1991): Does Ownership Always Matter ? International Journal of Industrial Organization 9, 55-72
33. European Bank for Reconstruction and Development (1997): Sound Business Standards and Corporate Practices. Working draft
34. Feldmann, R., Mehra, R. (1993): Auctions: Theory and Possible Applications to Economies in Transition. IMF Working Paper 93/12
35. Filatotchev, I., Wright, M., Buck, T. (1995): Corporate Governance and Voucher Buy-Outs in Russia. Annals of Public and Cooperative Economics 66/1, 77-99
36. Frydman, R., Pistor, K., Rapaczynski, A. (1996): Investing in Insider Dominated Firms - A study of Russian Voucher Privatization Funds. In Frydman, R., Grey, C., Rapaczynski, A. (Eds.): Corporate Governance in Central Europe and Russia Vol. 1. Central European University Press, 187-241
37. Frydman, R., Gray, C., Hessel, M., Rapaczynski, A. (1997): Private Ownership and Corporate Performance: Some Lessons Form Transition Economies. New York University Working Papers RR# 97-28
38. Glosten, L., Milgrom, P. (1985): Bid, Ask and Transaction Prices in a Specialist Market with Heterogeneously Informed Traders. Journal of Financial Economics 19, 71-100
39. Gomes, A. (1996): Going Public with Asymmetric Information, Agency Costs and Dynamic Trading. Harvard University mimeo
40. Gordon, M., Shapiro, E. (1956): Capital Equipment Analysis, the Required Rate of Profit. Management Science, 102-110
41. Grossman, S., Hart, O. (1980): Take-over Bids, the Free Rider Problem and the Theory of the Corporation. Bell Journal of Economics 11, 42-64
42. Hart, O. (1995): Corporate Governance: Some Theory and Implications. The Economic Journal 105, 678-689

43. Hart, O., Moore, J. (1990): Property Rights and the Nature of the Firm. Journal of Political Economy 98, 1119-1158

44. Hausman, J. (1981): Labour Supply. In Aaron, H. J., Pechman, J. (Eds.): How Taxes Affect Human Behaviour. Brookings Institution, 27-72

45. Holmstroem, B., Tirole, J. (1993): Market Liquidity and Performance Monitoring. Journal of Political Economy 101/4, 678-709

46. Holmstroem, B. (1982): Managerial Incentive Problems: A Dynamic Perspective. In Essays in Economics and Management in Honour of Lars Wahlbeck. Swedish School of Economics

47. International Finance Corporation (1995): Emerging Stock Markets Handbook

48. Jensen, M., Meckling, W. (1976): Theory of the Firm: Managerial Incentives, Agency Cost and Ownership Structure. Journal of Financial Economics 3, 305-360

49. Jenkinson, T., Mayer, C. (1994): The Costs of Privatization in the UK and France. In Bishop, M., Kay, J., Mayer, C. (Eds.): Privatization and Economic Performance. Oxford University Press, 290-298

50. Johnson, S., Loveman, G. (1995): Starting Over in Eastern Europe: Entrepreneurship and Economic Renewal. Harvard Business School Press

51. Kaufmann, D. (1996): The Missing Pillar of a Growth Strategy for the Ukraine: Institutional and Policy Reforms for Private Sector Development. Harvard Institute of International Development, mimeo

52. Kim, M., Koveos, P. (1994): Cross-Country Analysis of the Price-Earnings Ratio. Journal of Multinational Financial Management 3/4, 117-127

53. Klepach, A., Kuznetsov, P., Kryuchkova, P. (1996) Corporate Governance in Russia in 1995-1996. RECEP Working paper

54. Kocerba, J. (1996): Privatization and Restructuring: Friends or Enemies. CERGE Discussion Paper

55. Krasker, W. (1986): Stock Price Movements in Response to Stock Issues under Asymmetric Information. Journal of Finance 41/1, 93-105

56. Kyle, A. (1985): Continuous Auctions and Insider Trading. Econometrica 53/6, 1315-1335

57. Laffont, J.-J., Tirole, J. (1986): Using Cost Observation to Regulate Firms. Journal of Political Economy 94/3, 614-641

58. Laffont, J.-J., Tirole, J. (1991): Privatization and Incentives. The Journal of Law, Economics and Organization, Special edition V7, 84-105

59. La Porta, R., Lopez-de-Silanes, F., Shleifer, A., Vishny, R. (1996): Law and Finance. Harvard University Working Paper
60. La Porta, R., Lopez-de-Silanes, F., Shleifer, A., Vishny, R. (1997): Legal Determinants of External Finance. Harvard University Working Paper
61. Leland, H., Pyle, D. (1977): Informational Asymmetries, Financial Structure and Financial Intermediation. Journal of Finance 32/2, 371-387
62. Levy, H. (1982): Economic Valuation of Voting Power of Common Stock. Journal of Finance 38, 79-93
63. Mayer, C. (1989): Myths of the West: Lessons from Developed Countries for Development Finance. World Bank Discussion Paper
64. McMillan, J. (1995): Markets in Transition. Paper presented at the Seventh World Congress of the Econometric Society, Tokyo
65. Miller, M., Modigliani, F. (1961): Dividend Policy, Valuation and the of Shares. Journal of Business
66. Modigliani, F., Perotti, E. (1996): Protection of Minority Interest and the Development of Security Markets. MIT mimeo
67. Myers, C., Majluf, N. (1984): Corporate Financing and Investment Decisions: When Firms Have Information Investors do not Have. Journal of Financial Economics 13, 187-221
68. Nash, R., Willer, D. (1995): Share Prices in Russia: The Reasons for the Undervaluation. Russian Economic Trends 4/2, 89-127
69. Perotti, E. (1995): Credible Privatization. American Economic Review 85/4, 847-859
70. Pistor, K., Turkewitz, J. (1994): Coping with the Hydra - State Ownership after Privatization: A Comparative Analysis of Hungary, Russia and the Czech Republic. Paper for the joint conference of the World Bank and the Central European University Privatization Project
71. Pinto, B., Belka, M., Krajewski, S. (1993): Transforming State Enterprises in Poland: Evidence on Adjustment by Manufacturing Firms. Brookings Papers on Economic Activity 1, 213-270
72. Rinaco Plus (1997): Research Report R+, September 1997
73. Ravid, S., Sudit, E. (1994): Power Seeking Managers, Profitable Dividends and Financing Decisions. Journal of Economic Behavior and Organization 25, 241-255
74. Rock, K. (1986): Why New Issues are Underpriced. Journal of Financial Economics 15, 187-212

75. Roland, G. (1994): On the Speed and Sequencing of Privatization and Restructuring. Economic Journal 104, 1158-1168
76. Rose, R. (1995): New Russian Barometer IV: Survey Results. SPP Paper No. 250
77. Ross, S. A. (1977): The Determination of Financial Structure: The Incentive-Signalling Approach. Bell Journal of Economics, 134-139
78. Russian Economic Barometer. Institute of World Economy and International Relations, various issues
79. Russian Economic Trends. Whurr Publishers, various issues
80. Schmidt, K. (1996): The Costs and Benefits of Privatization: An Incomplete Contracts Approach. The Journal of Law, Economics and Organization V12N1, 1-24
81. Scholes, M., Williams, J. (1977): Estimating Betas from Nonsynchronous Data. Journal of Financial Economics 5, 309-327
82. Shleifer, A., Vasiliev, D. (1996): Management Ownership in Russian Privatization. In Frydman, R., Gray, C., Rapaczynski, A. (Eds.): Corporate Governance in Central Europe and Russia. CEU Press, 62-77
83. Shleifer, A., Vishny, R. (1986): Large Shareholders and Corporate Control. Journal of Political Economy 94/3, 461-479
84. Shleifer, A., Vishny, R. (1994): Politicians and Firms. Harvard Institute of Economic Research Discussion Paper No. 1686
85. Shleifer, A., Vishny, R. (1996): A Survey of Corporate Governance. NBER Working Paper 5554
86. Vickers, J., Yarrow, G. (1988): Privatization: An Economic Analysis. MIT Press
87. Willer, D., Nash, R. (1996): Reasons for the Low Valuation of Russian Shares. Economics of Transition 4/2, 449-457
88. Zingales, L. (1994): The Value of the Voting Right: a Study of the Milan Stock Exchange Experience. Review of Financial Studies 7, 125-148

Contributions to Economics

Hagen Bobzin
Indivisibilities
1998. ISBN 3-7908-1123-8

Helmut Wagner (Ed.)
Current Issues in Monetary Economics
1998. ISBN 3-7908-1127-0

Peter Michaelis/Frank Stähler (Eds.)
Recent Policy Issues in Environmental and Resource Economics
1998. ISBN 3-7908-1137-8

Jessica de Wolff
The Political Economy of Fiscal Decisions
1998. ISBN 3-7908-1130-0

Georg Bol/Gholamreza Nakhaeizadeh/
Karl-Heinz Vollmer (Eds.)
Risk Measurements, Econometrics and Neural Networks
1998. ISBN 3-7908-1152-1

Joachim Winter
Investment and Exit Decisions at the Plant Level
1998. ISBN 3-7908-1154-8

Bernd Meyer
Intertemporal Asset Pricing
1999. ISBN 3-7908-1159-9

Uwe Walz
Dynamics of Regional Integration
1999. ISBN 3-7908-1185-8

Michael Carlberg
European Monetary Union
1999. ISBN 3-7908-1191-2

Giovanni Galizzi/Luciano Venturini (Eds.)
Vertical Relationships and Coordination in the Food System
1999. ISBN 3-7908-1192-0

Batch number: 10725973

Printed by Printforce, the Netherlands